Subconscious Power

Subconscious Power

Use Your Inner Mind to Create the Life You've Always Wanted

———

Kimberly Friedmutter, CHt

ATRIA BOOKS

New York   London   Toronto   Sydney   New Delhi

ATRIA
BOOKS

An Imprint of Simon & Schuster, Inc.
1230 Avenue of the Americas
New York, NY 10020

Copyright © 2019 by KBF Entertainment LLC

All rights reserved, including the right to reproduce this book or portions thereof in any form whatsoever. For information, address Atria Books Subsidiary Rights Department, 1230 Avenue of the Americas, New York, NY 10020.

First Atria Books hardcover edition April 2019

ATRIA BOOKS and colophon are trademarks of Simon & Schuster, Inc.

For information about special discounts for bulk purchases, please contact Simon & Schuster Special Sales at 1-866-506-1949 or business@simonandschuster.com.

The Simon & Schuster Speakers Bureau can bring authors to your live event. For more information or to book an event, contact the Simon & Schuster Speakers Bureau at 1-866-248-3049 or visit our website at www.simonspeakers.com.

Interior design by Alexis Minieri

Manufactured in the United States of America

10 9 8 7 6 5 4 3 2 1

Library of Congress Cataloging-in-Publication Data

Names: Friedmutter, Kimberly, author.
Title: Subconscious power : use your inner mind to create the life you've always wanted / Kimberly Friedmutter, CHt.
Description: New York : Atria Books, [2019] | Includes bibliographical references and index. | Description based on print version record and CIP data provided by publisher; resource not viewed.
Identifiers: LCCN 2018047063 (print) | LCCN 2018049041 (ebook)
Subjects: LCSH: Hypnotism. | Subconsciousness. | Mental suggestion. | Change (Psychology)
Classification: LCC BF1156.S8 (ebook) | LCC BF1156.S8 F75 2019 (print) | DDC 154.7—dc23
LC record available at https://urldefense.proofpoint.com/v2/url?u=https-3A__lccn.loc.gov _2018047063&d=DwIFAg&c=jGUuvAdBXp_VqQ6t0yah2g&r=06HB5XcKNe3kUU36TuOk0fMyO_ eF5k6L7zVOIl7jYavLVBqUfi1IqLi0uMcjKSVc&m=XDHXmuSCOLyGkRQl6eBLO-v5WKOX- 6F2AlzusIj96hGI&s=kUlxCPhkKYZUlvuu0gmrCzgUYEyEM5bRMPH1znlUZRw&e=

ISBN 978-1-5011-8707-0
ISBN 978-1-5011-8709-4 (ebook)

This book is dedicated to my husband and soul-partner, Brad, who puts himself on the line every single day with humor and rich intelligence. His deep spirit, strong ethics, and moral compass are my model of soul-alignment. In a world of off-roading, he stays the course with wings, and I am grateful to fly alongside.

Contents

Part 2

Part 3

Subconscious Power

Introduction

The Power to Shape Your Life

What if I were to reveal an intuitive yet practical framework that cuts through the emotional and physical clutter obscuring your path, so that it becomes possible to envision the life you want and also make that vision real? What if you were to learn a set of simple, three-minute exercises that can alleviate pain, release you from resentment, and erase any residual shame you feel from past or present experiences? What if you were able to activate your own inner resources so that you could finally "play big" in your life without ever having to posture or pretend to be someone you're not?

Fully engaging in the marvelous creation of your own life is everyone's birthright. And yet few of us feel like we have the power to shape our own lives. Why do so few people believe they can get what they most want in life? Why do so many of us seem to fall short of our dreams? We get a taste of gratification and purpose, but then we watch, frustrated and helpless, as the momentous occasion or achievement seems to disappear, becoming a hazy memory. Just like going on a diet to lose weight for a big event and then watching as the pounds return with a vengeance, as if the weight is in control of your body, not you. Indeed, sometimes our own minds, bodies, and actions seem to work at cross purposes with our goals. Why is that?

The answer lies within you.

Subconscious Power makes the road to ultimate self-improvement accessible by showing you how to tap into a powerful force within you, a capacity for agency that you more than likely did not know you possessed. What is this mysterious power within? Your subconscious.

Your Inner Eight-Year-Old

The subconscious has been defined and referred to in many ways. The concept first emerged as a translation from the French word "subconscient," which was coined by the psychologist Pierre Janet (1859–1947) to refer to a "powerful awareness" that "lay underneath" conscious thought. A more mainstream definition that most people rely on is the thoughts and feelings that exist "below" the conscious mind. Indeed, ever since Freud popularized the term "subconscious" (which he later changed to the "unconscious"), psychologists and other theorists have gone back and forth without ever coming to a consensus about a preferred term, with some using "unconscious" and others, including myself, using "subconscious."

I prefer the term "subconscious" because it both offers a more positive connotation and feels more instinctive and closer to what we think of as intuition. Its power stems from the access the subconscious gives to our inner mind, which often knows more than we realize and always has a magical, elusive quality.

When you meet someone new and have an immediate sense of unease for no obvious reason, that's your subconscious talking to you. When something within you compels you to turn right instead of left on your usual route to the grocery store, that's also your subconscious talking. When you go on a job interview and come away with a feeling in every cell of your body that this is the opportunity you've spent your whole life waiting for—that's your subconscious. When you learn to attune yourself to this power and tap into its energy, the subconscious can then become your inner compass, guiding you to the life you truly desire and deserve.

I also refer to the subconscious as your inner eight-year-old. Why eight? Think about your eight-year-old self. He was old enough to think independently, yet young and innocent enough to listen to his true nature without worrying about what he was supposed to do or how he was supposed to act. If she didn't like her great-aunt, she wasn't going to pretend she did for the sake of family politics. In other words, eight is the age when we can articulate ideas and have opinions, but have not yet been overtaken by the vigilance of the conscious mind. The eight-year-old self speaks the truth frankly—exactly how she sees the world, without any interference from the expectations of others. He loves others without reserve and intuits the fact that we are all connected. Our inner eight-year-old relies on symbolism, takes everything personally, and is fully engaged in whatever activity is present at the time. But we age and mature, we silence the voice of our subconscious self; our eight-year-old grows up, disconnects from that inner voice of truth, and seems to disappear. In the pages ahead, you are going to not only find your subconscious; you will also reclaim its power.

Finding Your Long-Lost Self

We are at a point in our evolutionary cycle where we have become out of sync with our natures and need the subconscious more than ever. It's as if the more our brains become empowered—with information and knowledge—the louder the noise of the conscious mind, and the less access we have to the inner softness and enlightenment of our subconscious. Think about it: our lives are increasingly complex.

The technology that's designed to make our lives easier and more productive often leaves us feeling overwhelmed on a daily basis. At the same time, we've become separated from the natural world. This complicated, high-tech world has forced us to silence our subconscious and let our conscious selves take over. We have become too conscious, too driven, too obsessed. Where does this leave us? Disoriented, ungrounded, and stressed. We feel unbalanced, out of control, because we are disconnected from our subconscious, our inner, true self that knows best what we need to make us happy.

By tapping into your subconscious, as I'll show you how to do in this book, you will cut through the chaos and confusion of your daily life to know immediately, in the here and now, what you need—what your mind, body, and soul require—so that you can create the life you truly desire. All of us make choices during our lives and decisions that aren't in our best interest. My program is designed to teach you how to make choices that are positive and affirming.

Subconscious Power will unmask what's between you and the goals—big and small—that have thus far been out of your reach. By rediscovering your subconscious, allowing it to reveal itself and give you both permission and direction, you will learn how to get past obstacles that are keeping you from truly inheriting your birthright: a full, happy life shaped to your ultimate gratification. In the pages ahead, I will show you how to address and overcome the specific issues that are keeping you from living your best life. Depending on your individual needs and goals, you will learn to:

- Get past anxiety and depression
- Stop smoking
- Rein in out-of-control eating or drinking
- Lose weight, if that's your desire

- Let go of constant worries and fears that hold you in their grip
- Overcome procrastination
- Manage chronic pain
- Improve your memory
- Resolve sleep disturbances
- And so much more.

You may be wondering how one book, one program, can make so many different types of promises. That's just the thing: your subconscious contains the capacity for big problems and small challenges. It's a superpower that can adapt in scale to whatever you need it for. One of my clients, Matthew, a thirty-nine-year-old investment banker, was able to quit his twenty-five-year smoking habit. Lori, a forty-two-year-old former model, was able to reduce bloating steroid medicines she'd been taking to manage pain related to fibromyalgia. Kendra, a sixty-year-old art dealer, described living a life free of the crippling anxiety that had been keeping her like a prisoner in her own home. Throughout the book, you will meet other clients who have used my approach to solve physical and emotional problems that had been holding them back from not only living full, satisfying lives but also from achieving their fullest potential.

My Life's Work

Bringing people back into balance has been my life's work. As a board-certified, registered hypnotherapist, I have used my rigorous training in hypnosis and neuro-linguistic programming (NLP) to help people solve everyday problems that constrain their abilities and hold them back from truly experiencing and enjoying the full potential of their lives. My work with women and men of all ages and backgrounds is based most generally on the tradition of Ericksonian hypnotherapy (founded by Milton Erickson, MD); however, it is also supported by substantive research in neuroscience, cognitive science, positive psychology, and Gestalt therapy. Over a twenty-year career as a certified hypnotherapist and life management consultant, I have worked with all sorts of people—world-renowned actors and actresses, sports stars, millionaires and billionaires. I've learned that these people, for all their fame and fortune, are exactly like the rest of us. They share the same problems, challenges, and obstacles in their lives. Problems that you would assume stardom, wealth, and access to anything they could ever want would keep at bay. But you would be wrong.

Every one of us is like a car or other machine. And everyone's car has had some mechanical malfunction at some point in time. Now imagine a car that ages as we all do. Chances are, any problems, if unaddressed, will get worse with time, regardless of how much money you make and how famous you are. Your thoughts, both conscious and subconscious, are vulnerable to mechanical issues and anxiety. Depression. Addiction. Fear. Loneliness. Low self-esteem. Weight gain. Chronic illness. Disease. Relationship conflict. These are ordinary problems that can take hold of our lives, blocking our path, ruining our chances of making our dreams come true, and, in many ways, undermining our health and happiness.

Hypnosis can offer men and women relief and release from various problems, in varying degrees of severity. Some people need to heal from past traumas. Others must get over failed relationships in order to meet a suitable mate. Other women and men come to me to lose unwanted weight that has completely consumed their vision of themselves and swallowed their hopes and beliefs in their own potential. Many clients start their journey by learning new ways to manage their anxiety, depression, and other emotional issues. Others finally achieve lasting weight loss. Still other people come to a place of clarity and wholeness when they realize that their social or romantic entanglements are keeping them from success in other aspects of their lives—professional, creative, or spiritual. And still others, who may have reached massive success in one realm, come to discover, through accessing the power of their subconscious, even more satisfaction in another arena: a new career, for instance.

Mining the resources of your subconscious ultimately brings you supreme agency over your life. Agency is that capacity that enables us to actively shape our lives instead of being a passive participant. The Six Principles of Subconscious Power are designed to give you the inner tools to build and harness agency, which culminate in the final principle: the ability to play big. Indeed, *Subconscious Power* takes the work I do with my clients—and the very process I use for myself—and makes it accessible and attainable for you in your life. Using the insight into how hypnosis works and exercises I designed to deepen the exploration of the subconscious, you will give yourself the gift of learning who you are and who you can become. You will remove the obstacles that are in your way and connect to your own superpower.

Zone Out to *Really* Zone In

The trance state of hypnosis has the power to deliver almost instant insight and clarity. There's a lot of focus on mindfulness these days, but my approach is different, and in many ways simpler: it asks you to zone out instead of zoning in. Because trance is an innate state (more on this in a minute), you don't need any special equipment to access it; indeed, it's a natural extension of your subconscious power. All you will need is awareness and a willingness to act; and the exercises in this book (I call them Hypnotic Hacks) are designed to help you do exactly that.

You can use trance to upend your current status quo and get what you really want and truly deserve. This program will teach you to quickly tap into your own subconscious so that you can cut through the minutia of everyday life, let go of common yet false beliefs, and stop settling for a mediocre life; you can aspire to and achieve a *great* life, the big life, the life you deserve.

My clients are amazed when they realize how easy it is to let go of their habits of self-sabotage and the stress that comes with a seemingly never-ending to-do list. That's the magical part of *Subconscious Power*: it allows you to easily release your distractions and worries so that you can experience your life more fully. So that you are not just surviving life, but surviving successfully. So that instead of living a life constrained by doubts and fears of isolation, you discover one in which all your relationships feel copacetic and supportive, energizing and reciprocal.

Some people may still carry an inaccurate impression of hypnosis or believe they are "just not suggestible." Still others are afraid of where they might "go" when being hypnotized. This book will address these misconceptions and clarify, for good, how hypnosis and its practices can lead to remarkable transformation. As if holding a torch to illuminate the path, I help my clients find their way out of the darkness, rise above hopelessness, and continue past the obstacles that block their way. Most issues are simply imagined scary shadows created by long-gone skeletons or stubborn but untrue beliefs that still go bump in the night, years after we consciously know better. This book will connect you to your subconscious and a vast source of energy and light that will help you cut through the clutter that is dragging you down and offer you ease, abundance, and so much more.

Through my work, I've seen many lives turned around in big and small ways. By connecting to their subconscious, my clients have learned to discern between what's real and what's not; what matters and what doesn't; what's necessary and what's dispensable—one ladder rung at a time. Every step they take elevates them to the next level of understanding and enlightenment about themselves and the power they have to change their lives. You will read their stories, observe their transformations, and, I hope, be inspired to create the life you want.

How the Program Works

This book shares Six Principles designed to illuminate your subconscious and activate it. These principles are based on truths that have emerged from my years of working with all types of people, coupled with powerful hypnotherapeutic techniques. Just like my clients, you can use these principles and exercises to excavate what's not working in your life and connect to your subconscious self. It's the subconscious that enables all of us to know exactly what to do. Once we learn to listen to our subconscious, it can guide us to the life we truly desire.

When I work one-on-one with clients, I guide them into a relaxed hypnotic state (nothing in the world feels as good as trance). I then ask questions that prompt them to reveal themselves to me and to themselves, a process of self-revelation that is both healing and transformative.

The principles and exercises in this book will do the same for you, acting as a form of self-hypnosis that you can use in your daily life. You might think of these three-minute hypnotic hacks as mini lessons. They are not strenuous, though they may be challenging at first. They do not require you to commit to years of therapy—who has time for that? These exercises are designed to give you less to do and think about consciously. By tuning into the subconscious, you give your tired conscious mind a much-needed break. This is the master plan of *Subconscious Power*: using your own capacity for trance and connecting with your inner eight-year-old, you will quiet the too-loud voice of your conscious mind so you can once again hear your subconscious. Indeed, you will feel like you work less hard, yet get more in return.

Part 1, "The Hidden Potential of Your Subconscious," explains the Six Principles and shares key hypnotic hacks to help you tap into the wisdom of your subconscious. These hacks work for you in two important ways: they help you become aware of the powerful energy of your subconscious, which in turn helps prepare you to balance your overwrought conscious mind. The more adept you become at communicating with your subconscious, the more you will learn how to use its spontaneous focus and cogent insight to tamp down the controlling, overthinking conscious mind. I affectionately refer to the conscious mind as the Critical Thinker because of its tendency to get caught up in the minutiae of decision-making, trying to exert control over all the details of everyday life. Indeed, the Critical Thinker can often lead to so much anxiety, we end up falling into a well of analysis-paralysis.

In addition to the subconscious and the conscious mind, you will also learn about another dimension to this program: what I refer to as your SoulSpirit. Think of the SoulSpirit as God, your inner divinity, or your connection to the spiritual realm. This dimension is highly personal, as we all differ in our spiritual beliefs; however, its presence is not only ubiquitous but infinite because it connects you to the wider universe. Throughout the book, you will encounter reminders to connect to your SoulSpirit, which reinforces your access to your subconscious and seals your everlasting connection with the universe as a whole. Ultimately, by the end of the book, you will come full circle and learn hacks that will connect you directly to the energy of the Soul-Spirit.

In each of the chapters of part 1, you will use the Six Principles to facilitate the changes you want in your life—some of these shifts might be related to negative or self-defeating thought patterns or behaviors; some might be related to the relationships in your life that need recalibration. And although the Six Principles appear in a particular order, as do the Hypnotic Hacks, they ultimately can be used in any way that appeals to you. You may also find yourself returning to certain hacks again and again.

The chapters in part 2, "Master Your Best Life," zero in on specific issues that can undermine your subconscious power or leave your subconscious and your conscious mind out of proper balance. You will use new hacks in tandem with the ones you learned in part 1 to troubleshoot life's inevitable challenges, including how to get out of drought, that state of negativity that can separate you from your subconscious; how to support and nourish your body so that it can do its best work for you; and how to heal old wounds and restore your relationships. All of us, at one time or another, have been disappointed—in our bodies, our minds, our hearts, our relationships, our life experiences. Any pain or discomfort, regardless of its degree of trauma, creates a fragmentation and separation from who we truly are, distancing us from our subconscious. In these chapters, you will learn how to connect these fragments so the awareness you developed through the Six Principles can deliver you into your new life.

Finally, in part 3, "Leap of Faith," you will come to understand that life is not a line, but a loop. In other words, by connecting with those loved ones who have passed away (a state of transformation that I refer to as "transitioned"), you will reinforce your SoulSpirit connection. Like the universal principle of the conservation of energy, we never cease existing; we simply change form. Think of how ice changes from solid to liquid to water vapor under the influence of temperature. I believe that life has no end, just constant beginnings.

As you work through the Six Principles, I also suggest you jot down notes—not to chronicle your process—again, I want this whole book to feel easy-breezy. Rather, putting down your thoughts and feelings as you move through the chapters and exercises will keep you tapped into your subconscious in a spectacular way. As you nurture your relationship with this inner self, you will be able to accomplish small feats with ease: set daily goals and achieve them; create more time to truly relax; get along better with the people in your life; leverage your strengths to get what you want.

An Easier Path

Before beginning this process, I want you to know one thing about me: I've walked this journey myself. I've made my share of mistakes, gotten off course with the wrong people at the wrong times, and believed that life had to be a battle. I was brought up to believe all the clichés: no pain, no gain; no guts, no glory; and other lies about value. But it was not until I discovered hypnotherapy that I was able to heal and move past beliefs, habits, and behaviors that were keeping me in my own dark cave. Hypnosis taught me I didn't have to struggle, didn't have to become tough as nails or hard as metal in order to succeed. In other words, through hypnosis I learned that *life isn't a battle, so I don't have to make it one.*

Like me, this process is grounded in reality, but aimed at getting you to the stars. You know that phrase, "I love you to the moon and back"? That's the channel we're on. The Six Principles can take you from the grass in your garden to Jupiter, from the sea to stratospheric Saturn, from beer to bubbly champagne—all while you are becoming the real, super-improved you. It's not time travel, but *soul* travel. My mission is to show you how to use your journey to your best advantage. Your future can evolve as big and wide as the ocean and as endless as the sky. And I will show you how to get there.

You will, however, need to show up—not for me, but for yourself. You will need to be honest when you look at yourself. You will need to allow room for the truth, so the truth can appear with clarity. With the truth on your side, no matter how scary, uncertain, or threatening situations in your life may seem, you will create a happier life, a life of learnings and the love you truly deserve.

Are you ready?

1

The Hidden Potential
of Your Subconscious

Chapter 1

A Return to Your Pure State

"The most important thing you can do on this planet—elevate, transform and illuminate your own consciousness."

—CARLOS SANTANA

We've all experienced something spectacular in our lives. Just now, bring it to mind. When it happened, did you feel like the stars had aligned? The universe had delivered? The magnetic energies of the poles had met? Did you feel the presence or existence of God, karma, or a powerful energy source? Did you feel whole and connected to the universe in a larger, tangible way?

What if that pull, that call, that force was not somewhere *outside* you, but *inside* you all along? That power is your subconscious; and when you are connected to your subconscious, you tap into a deep energy source, a power that is within you, just waiting to be released. In the pages ahead, I will teach you how to access your subconscious, the mother of all motherboards, and discover how to tap into the biological circuitry that runs our bodies, our breath, our deepest thoughts. The Six Principles of Subconscious Power will be your guide, your tool kit for solving everyday problems and accessing a greater sense of control over your own life. This control is called agency, and it's key to learning how to play big and create the life you want, the life of your dreams.

How I Discovered Hypnosis

I discovered the power of my subconscious through my personal experience with hypnosis. Though I've always had strong intuition, my trust in the power of hypnosis deepened and expanded when I trained to become a certified hypnotherapist. This formal training enabled me to listen to and nurture this inner voice and pay attention to its wisdom. And then I began to change as a result. My hard-driven, conscious self stopped operating in overdrive and began to quiet down. Fine-tuning my relationship with my own subconscious also allowed me a new level of awareness, and I saw myself and the world around me with new, fresh eyes. The best part? I realized that this mind-shift was completely sustainable, 100 percent organic, and seemingly effortless. Suddenly, I realized that my goals—my hopes and dreams—were right in front of me all along. Before, I had been running too hard for lift-off, not knowing how to engage my wings; the subconscious enabled me to soar.

What did this personal transformation look like?

Before I discovered my own subconscious power, I was unsatisfied with my life. I was reactive to everything, a chameleon constantly changing myself to fit the circumstances. I was motivated to be all things to all people, overextending, overgiving, and not truly trusting of myself or others. I treated all my relationships as if they were transactions, leading with my penchant for organization and what would work best in a *professional* environment. I believed that the visual tension between my soft, hyperfeminine appearance and my success at a major FM talk-radio station in Los Angeles set me apart from others in the highly competitive LA dating pool.

What I didn't quite understand was how I was a kind of walking contradiction, even to myself. I had been raised in the South, where it was very important to be quiet and ladylike, and, yes, submissive as well. At the same time, southern girls were also expected to be strong and reliable, but not to show this resilience on the exterior. And since I was blessed with good looks and height, I naturally fell into an early modeling career that gave me my first taste of success . . . and a reliance on my appearance. The result? I learned how to use my beauty as income, literally taking my "face value" as a commodity.

This all may seem glamorous—at fourteen, I was working abroad and had been signed with several world-class modeling agencies—but even then, I knew something was missing.

Luckily, I had a strong head on my shoulders and was determined to study while I traveled in foreign countries. Also, being independent at such a young age forced me to learn other survival skills: I became a careful and astute observer of people, learning the ways of the world by watching how the adults around me acted and reacted, made decisions and mistakes.

Flash-forward a decade or so. I landed in Los Angeles and continued modeling for a bit, then got involved in acting. I continued to hone my curiosity about human behavior, listening to those around me, taking in information about how the world works and how people got what they wanted. This passion for people developed into a career as a radio talk show host for one of the largest stations in the LA area. On the surface, my life was on a roll.

But as we know, all that glitters is not gold. Despite my very real outward success, I was still conflicted. This conflict was most evident in my romantic relationships, which were tumultuous and ultimately unhappy. Instead of attracting a mate who would see me as a woman and a partner, I drew highly accomplished men in need of a life manager and organizer. By default, I wound up playing the role of the controlling person in the relationship. I often found myself "going

General," getting the job done, but plowing over people in the process. I was scary, not sexy. Yes, I felt strong and in control, but I was far from happy. What I really wanted was to be more soft and receptive as opposed to assertive; and yes, I wanted to be taken care of and valued for who I was—not as arm candy. (A lot of men would like to feel this way, too; this feeling is not gender-specific.) My outer shell was just that—a protective exterior that could crack at any moment. For all my bravado and "get it done" efficiency, I was cut off from my true strength within.

My relationship with John was a perfect example. He certainly wasn't my only failed relationship, but he was the last one, the one that finally freed me from a bad cycle and put me on my path to the love I have today. John was an entertainment industry power player who was lean but not too lean, with an infectious smile. He was known to have his eyes on the prize; he didn't allow himself to become distracted by relationship drama or anything too far afield from being a successful businessman and making a lot of money. I admired his ambition and his desire for success, and I was attracted to his laser focus and commitment to work.

For his part, John adored me because—in his words—I seemed to have it "all together." He told me that he needed a "real" partner who could understand his world and thrive right alongside him. In other words, I looked the part and played it well.

Our relationship worked for a time. Publicly, I was John's glamorous right hand when we socialized, smoothly providing confidence and southern charm. I was also the supreme organizer of his life, happy to take up the reins and release him from social and family responsibilities. I managed his personal office, his staff, and his children—I basically ran his day-to-day life. Privately, I was his go-to support, offering him guidance based on my work with human behavior, practically tucking him in at night with reassurance on many occasions. And, boy, did he like and need what I was giving. John thrived under my care.

One night, all this changed. Late in the evening, as I was getting ready for a busy next day, I passed through a room adjoining the one John was in and I happened to hear snippets of the conversation he was having. I actually thought he was talking to me, since he was speaking in a tone that sounded like pillow talk, a voice and cadence reserved for me, his lover. What caught my attention was not his words, but his tone, and I couldn't stop listening. He wasn't whispering, but he was confiding in someone. To whom was he talking in this manner, so private and intimate?

I soon realized he was talking *about* me. And then I heard him use the dreaded C-word to describe me: *controlling*. I felt immediate rage—and also embarrassment, shame, and fear. I was reeling! If all my efforts to make John happy had resulted in his feeling that I was an overbearing shrew, then I had failed us both.

My defenses kicked in, and my thoughts lashed back. *If he would just man up, I wouldn't have to be so* controlling *and play so many roles, including that of his mother.* But no matter how defensive I felt, I kept coming back to one particular fact that I could not deny: this wasn't the first time I'd been called the C-word. Suddenly and for the first time, I saw very clearly how my ingrained need to please and to support other people (men especially) had turned me into a hard-charging, controlling superwoman who had lost sight of my inner softness. Who had I become?

Not only had I acted in this way with men before, I had also taken this approach in many of my other relationships—with family, friends, and people I worked with. I suddenly saw my role in yet another failed relationship with crystal clarity and felt *exhausted*. I couldn't look at John when he hung up the phone. I didn't even worry about whom he was talking to. *I* had heard it, and that was horrific enough.

I had some soul-searching to do. Who was I if I wasn't running,

helping, and hurdling all of John's—or any partner's—needs? What did
it say about me that I had attracted yet another person who wanted me
to be a "package" rather than a person? This was my pattern. Why did
I choose an opportunist rather than someone truly invested in me? I
also wondered, what had I really been attracted to in John? Had I seen
him as a project? Before I could find the love I wanted, I had to face
these questions and others head-on. As tempting as it was, I couldn't
blame John; I could only try to understand myself and why I had chosen John and the other men before him.

In search of some help, I sought out hypnosis. I'd been hypnotized
many years before, and now I was even more curious about how this
process might help me. I had a gut feeling that part of the reason I was
enacting this deeply ingrained pattern again and again in my life was
because I was not in touch with my subconscious: I was not even conscious of how I'd been acting. Why was I continually behaving in ways
that undermined my own happiness? So I began hypnotherapy, and
decided later to go deeper and engage in professional training.

Through hypnosis, I was able to confront my actions, dissect my
own behavior patterns and relationship dynamics, and learn to love
through my softness, not my efficiency and need to control. I had to let
go of my inner "General" so I could welcome the real me.

In hindsight, John was able to be the man I longed for—happy, relaxed, and lucky—only because he had had me running his messy life.
I was treating him the way I wanted to be treated, but not expecting the
same care in return. In doing so, I ensured that our relationship didn't
stand a chance. It did not have the balance of power and energy so critical to all healthy relationships: I was giving more than I was getting,
a resentful dynamic that will eventually undermine any relationship.

I once said of this time in my life that I felt like a forceful four-
hundred-pound bouncer standing outside a rowdy underground night-

ind, along with energy and wisdom that guide me to make
hat support me, my health, and my happiness. And as I grew
ence in my subconscious power, I also found I was able to
ulSpirit, that vast source of spirit-centered energy that per-
e universe. The more I dove into my hypnosis training, un-
ng its nuances and depths, the more I came to understand
e SoulSpirit that helps cement the alignment of the subcon-
d the conscious mind. When the two sides of ourselves are in
e subconscious and the conscious—something magical hap-
attune ourselves to the universe in a new, deeper way. It's as
n up another channel of understanding and experience the
und us in a heightened state of awareness.

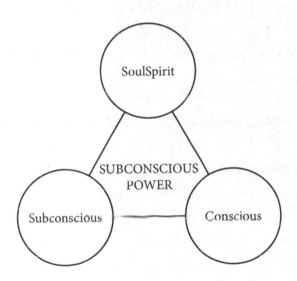

s more sensitive awareness begins with tuning into the subcon-
indeed, our subconscious is the conduit that enables us to have
rocal relationship with the universe: we give out positive energy,
e receive it back from the universe.
is way of connecting to my subconscious has had another sur-

club. Internally, I felt like a brute. I had
attracting and creating relationships th
needed only happened when I finally w
I was headed and tapped into the truth:
go neutral. I was going to get further sit

I understood with clarity that *on*
age, and love, but what did I want? In
health, a devoted husband, a life of laug
to magical places. I wanted wealth on ev
physical, and financial—just as if I'd ma
that I wanted and asked the universe to i

By assessing myself honestly—warts
essary next steps, I got my dream, and so

How did I get it?

I created a path for myself that has no
ciples of this book:

- I acknowledged how I had created
  my life.
- I reconnected with my subconsciou
- I learned tools that allowed me to b
  subconscious and my conscious mi
- I cleared my path of false beliefs and
- I learned how to ask for what I want
- I created the energy to go for it.

Eventually, these steps that I took myself
Six Principles, and through them, along with
ration of my own subconscious power, I learn
From this state of clarity and strength, I

peace of n
decisions
this confi
trust in S
meates th
derstandi
that it's t
scious an
sync—th
pens: we
if we op
world ar

Th
scious
a reci
and w
T

prising effect: I realized that I could trust my softness and recover my innate femininity, that my softness wasn't my weakness—she was my strength. I could let go of all the defensive postures of my four-hundred-pound bouncer and the brash battle cries that I used to believe were necessary in order to achieve my goals. Together, my inner eight-year-old and my Critical Thinker would show me the way, if I would just tuck in and listen, quiet down, and stay receptive. I would finally get back to the real me. This applies, of course, to men, too, who know all too well the frustration, limitations, and negative consequences of a pounding fist. True power whispers; it doesn't scream.

Trance: Zone Out!

Hypnosis is easy. In fact, trance is a natural state of being. Every time you get lost in the music when your favorite artist sings your favorite song, that's trance. When large groups of fans move in sync at a concert, they are in a trance state. When you find yourself mesmerized, staring out a window or into your refrigerator, unable to turn away—that's trance. This is the natural state of your inner eight-year-old.

When we are at rest, zoned out or daydreaming, we are lulled in trance. It feels good, right? It feels good for a reason: because trance is our nature. Remember, as a child, suddenly coming into consciousness when the teacher got the class's attention by snapping her fingers or tapping the blackboard? As children we are natural daydreamers for a reason: we are still tied intimately to our subconscious. And yet not all people lose this thread to their subconscious after childhood. Creative people—scientists, artists, inventors—have spoken about how daydreaming brought on their biggest insights, innovations, and discoveries. A study published in 2017 in the journal *Neuropsychologia* found a correlation between people who daydream frequently and higher intelligence and creativity. By scanning the brains of study participants using fMRI, researchers were able to link the awake resting state of daydreaming with higher scores on analytic and creative tasks. So next time, let your "mental diversions" roll! As you will see in chapter 3, your inner eight-year-old loves to let their mind wander.

While my story about John represents just one aspect of my own transformative journey, it shows the power of hypnosis to shift you from one way of being and living to another. Understanding how hypnosis works as a vehicle for change and transformation requires you to do two things: 1) *accept* the Six Principles of subconscious power that enable you to expel false beliefs, shift limiting behaviors, and ultimately move into habits of mind that activate agency; and 2) *take a leap of faith* by acting on those principles.

Dr. Milton Erickson was one of the first clinicians to have extensively researched hypnotherapy and documented the resulting positive effects. Working during the 1950s and '60s, Erickson used an approach that emphasized the individual nature of any type of therapeutic work, stressing that just one theory or approach was inconsistent with the nature of human beings. Given his own physical limitations (he was almost entirely paralyzed from polio), Erickson paid close attention to how we use nonverbal communication (body language and tone of voice, for example) to reveal what we might otherwise not express. He captured and described the experience of hypnotherapy, cataloguing hundreds of patients who made significant emotional and physical transformations through the tools of hypnosis, including indirect suggestion, the use of metaphors, and storytelling. Erickson was one of the first medical experts to show the real, concrete benefits of hypnosis and demonstrate its scientific foundation through his research.

Since then, hypnotherapy has become a standard practice among psychiatrists and psychotherapists, especially those who adhere to the belief that much of our behavior, thoughts, and feelings can be explained by processes that are below the level of conscious awareness. In my experience, people can make subtle yet profound changes through the power of suggestion—both direct and indirect—that forms the basis of the interaction between hypnotist and participant. As you will see in the pages ahead, my hypnotherapy clients have lost weight, overcome paralyzing fears, healed rifts in their relationships, decreased chronic pain, and more.

Another way to appreciate the benefits of hypnotherapy and the principles of subconscious power is to see how they function similarly to meditation. Just as meditation has been used for centuries in Eastern cultures as a method for accessing a state of enlightenment and transcendence, hypnotherapy also provides a way to harness the power of the universe and bring it into the sphere of the individual. Indeed, modern neuroscientists including Richard Davidson and Antonio Damasio have shown quantifiable benefits of meditation to promote not only greater mindfulness (Davidson defines mindfulness as "the practice of nonjudgmental, moment-to-moment awareness") but also concrete health benefits, including the reduction of psychological distress and the lifting of depression. Indeed, Jon Kabat-Zinn, a Buddhist scholar and medical doctor, created the mindfulness-based stress reduction (MBSR) program, which is based on the measurable outcomes of meditation. MBSR is now a widely used approach and program, consisting of an eight-week workshop that includes mindfulness meditation, body awareness, and yoga.

Hypnotherapy has also shown these stress-reducing benefits, as well as effectiveness for quitting smoking, pain management during and after surgery, and improvement in memory functioning, among many other positive effects. In a 2000 article published in the *International Journal of Experimental Hypnosis*, several psychological researchers detailed an extensive analysis of numerous clinical studies, including their own, validating the effectiveness of hypnosis for the treatment of a number of mental and physical ailments. One seminal study, conducted by psychologists Steven Lynn, PhD, Irving Kirsch, PhD, Arreed Barabasz, PhD, Etzel Cardeña, PhD, and David Patterson, PhD, demonstrated that hypnosis is particularly effective for reduction of pain. (See References on page 247 for additional studies.)

However, there is a very key difference between meditation and the process I describe here: meditation wants you to sharpen your awareness and become *mind-ful*; I'm asking you to zone out—let your mind wander so that in trance, you can hear, see, and feel what your subconscious has in store for you. And this is where the leap of faith comes in. Trance is immeasurable and mysterious. It is real and yet experienced as almost a haze of awareness.

As Miriam, a forty-two-year-old client, describes, "I thought being hypnotized would make me feel kind of sedated, too relaxed. But it was the opposite. I felt so much more motivated. I had more energy for what I wanted to do."

Brian, a fifty-eight-year-old physician, shared this with me: "I was a skeptic. As a medical doctor, hypnosis seemed like fluff. But when I was finally able to lose twenty pounds and my sleeplessness disappeared, I became a believer. I'm not a very religious person, but now I truly believe that there's more to reality than meets the naked eye. I used to wake up constantly throughout the night—now I can sleep through like a baby."

This book is not a training manual that teaches you how to hypnotize others; the process you are about to begin is more like a form of self-hypnosis. The principles and exercises will teach you how to access the trance state and connect you to your subconscious power;

these ideas and activities build on one another, enabling you to grow your subconscious power and lead you to the ultimate expression of agency—playing big in your life.

In so doing, you will discover a sense of peace and serenity, renewed energy, and sharpened focus. The more you're able to access this trance state and listen to your subconscious, the more you will discover a clear sense of agency and deeper insight into yourself and others. You will create relationships that work better for you. You will give yourself the opportunity to rise above the fray of everyday living and evolve into your biggest, boldest self.

The beauty of using exercises based on these time-tested methods of hypnosis and hypnotherapy is that they work on the ground level of our lives, giving us tools to make our daily lives clearer and richer. Think of an old, rusty car. The exercises and principles in this book are designed to help you feel cleaned up, buffed up, and shined up so that you sparkle. The contrasting gleam of newly polished metal? That's how small changes can make such enormous impacts.

I like to say that this learning process helps you become who you are ultimately meant to be. Indeed, that is the purpose, and the promise, of this book. Are you ready to create the life you've always wanted?

Activating the Six Principles of Your Subconscious Power

Tapping into your subconscious will enable you to bring your conscious self, your Critical Thinker, into alignment, so that it does not interfere or overwork. The conscious mind or Critical Thinker is that voice in your head that drives your decisions and your actions, and stays often stubbornly attached to unhelpful ways of being. Of course, we need our conscious mind to make effective, productive decisions, but with its tendency to micromanage the little things and rationalize our behavior, it often separates us from who we really are and what will ultimately make us happy. In other words, the subconscious, our true self, knows the real source of our happiness; our conscious mind, the Critical Thinker, often stays attached to superficial or ephemeral sources of happiness. Learning how to reignite your relationship with your subconscious and align it with your conscious mind allows you to inhabit your authentic, complete self.

From this place of balance, you then call upon and receive the energy of the SoulSpirit, in a more immediate, impactful way. The Soul-Spirit can mean many different things to each of us. Some people may think of God, Buddha, Jehovah, Allah, or angels. Others might feel a divinity within. Others experience the soul or spirit as energy that connects us to nature or the universe. Perhaps you've felt this connection in a religious service, or in a moment when you've been overcome by the beauty of nature. How you define this dimension is up to you, but growing your relationship with your subconscious asks you to call upon this dimension regularly so that you can infuse your life with the energy of the universe. The awesomeness of looking at the vastness of the night sky, a stand of trees within a forest, or the backdrop of mountains can elicit feelings associated with magnificence, sacredness, or splendor. So, too, can the birth of a child, an intense yoga or meditation practice, or the pure love of another person. Ushering in the SoulSpirit requires a leap of faith and answering the call to a higher sensibility, one that may not be concrete or visible, but one that I imagine you will be willing to experience once you move through the program.

The Six Principles that I discovered are based on universal practices and elements of hypnosis that enable you to quickly and regularly tap into and draw on the strength of your subconscious. You will learn how to enter trance and benefit from this state, and to use this primal insight to make more strategic, rewarding decisions. Again, trance is your natural state, your "screensaver mode," where you relax, meditate, create, imagine, and rise to your full potential. In this state of awareness, you will then come to learn how to use your subconscious to calm and direct your conscious mind, bringing these two dimensions into balance so that you can think more clearly, feel more centered, and be more wholly yourself.

Remember, the principles are laid out in the order that most people use them when starting this process, as there is an organic progression that occurs. However, you can really choose to begin at whichever principle makes the most sense to you. Indeed, I ask you throughout the principles to assess where you are, so that you can continually hone your own self-awareness. This tuning into how you are thinking and feeling is important to maximizing the benefits of the process.

Here are the Six Principles of Subconscious Power:

- **Principle One: Come into Accountability**—You will learn to be nakedly honest with yourself so that you can become accountable for who you are, what you want, and where you've been. In other words, own who you are right now, with all your baggage, faults, mistakes, and glimpses of imperfections. This composite is the *real* you. Before you can access your subconscious directly, you want a clean slate.

- **Principle Two: Tap into Your Subconscious Power**— You will learn to activate your subconscious so that you can grow your intuitive knowledge of yourself and bring your conscious mind into alignment. This basic building block of my approach has many access points; you will find numerous exercises to help you tap into your subconscious.

- **Principle Three: Move Toward or Away**—Our actions speak louder than words. You will learn to assess how you respond to situations and people in either of two ways: by approaching a situation or by retreating or avoiding it. Understanding your orientation gives you a heightened sense of self-awareness, an important building block for growing your subconscious power.

- **Principle Four: Judge Thyself and Thy Neighbor**—Hearing the subconscious clearly requires that we use the good judgment of the subconscious, instead of resorting to the overly reactive or biased decisions made by an overtaxed conscious mind. In addition, by using our relationships as a lens, we can practice the good judgment of our subconscious to keep us on our path.

- **Principle Five: Give to Get**—Getting what you want from life means accepting that you are entitled to get it. And attaining your dreams and well-deserved happiness depends, in part, on how well you can leverage opportunities and situations in your life. This "golden principle" of the subconscious is like a secret passage to get what you want, all while you honor the highest part of another person.

- **Principle Six: Play Big**—In this final principle, you will assume the posture that will make your goals, dreams, and aspirations come into reality. Do you want a happier relationship? Do you want a new career? Do you want to stop procrastinating or worrying so much? Do you simply want to like yourself more? Whatever your wish, you will come to name it and go for it. This principle brings your subconscious into full alignment with your conscious mind and the collective energy of the universe so that you can make real your smallest and biggest of goals.

The Big Picture

When used together, the Six Principles give you a path to enlightenment and heightened self-awareness. Activating your subconscious will enable you to feel whole, unencumbered, and free to be who you are meant to be. As you do so, keep in mind the ultimate goal of joining the energy and wisdom of your subconscious with your conscious mind and the SoulSpirit. These three elements need to work together in harmony in order for you to lead the life you ultimately desire and deserve. It's the job of the subconscious to channel your inner eight-year-old so you can stay true to your best self. It's the job of your conscious mind to draw on the wisdom of the subconscious and make sure that the way you are living and being is in your true best interest. It's the job of the SoulSpirit to infuse your being with light and truth, by regularly calling upon the immeasurable vastness and energy of the universe. This book will help you weave the three threads of self-awareness, conscious mind, and SoulSpirit together to enable you to come into your full potential.

The process is inherently flexible and naturally iterative. In other words, the principles and their exercises can work immediately, but most people, including myself, benefit from returning to them again and again as our lives change and we continue to adapt and evolve. Indeed, every time you repeat these exercises, you create more opportunities for positive outcomes. Just like physical exercise, the more frequent the practice, the better your results. You can return to the exercises and principles of the subconscious again and again, always with a fresh start, a new wish, and a clean slate.

And since they work quickly and efficiently, you don't have to overthink the how, when, or where. You will see that all the Hypnotic Hacks begin in the same way: "Close your eyes and go within." This direction acts as a trigger for entering trance and readying your mind and body for the upcoming experience. In the beginning, you may want to establish a special place in your home for this ritual; however, these exercises are designed to be done anywhere, at any time—in bed, at your desk, or even while working out.

Here's another way to think of this process: Have you ever sat down to a meal, thinking you weren't hungry, only to realize, after the first bite, that you were famished? Have you woken up in the middle of the night with the solution to a tricky problem, one you didn't even realize you were trying to work out? You may think you're fine, hanging in there just like everyone else, but understand that you are one bite away from realizing your next goal. And that is what you will experience as you read on—just like me, that night when I overheard John's conversation, and just like every client I have worked with throughout my career. Once you wake up to how you really feel, you won't want to wait to make the necessary changes to be all you want to be and get all that you need. The time is now. The relief is now. Satiety is within your reach. There is no more waiting. What you want in life is all up to you. Identify your own dreams—however big or small, short-term or long-term.

By showing up here and now, I know you are ready to be nourished, excited, and fed. You are ready to shine a torch on your own path out of the cave of unknowing, to travel forward with wisdom and courage.

Where Are You Now?

I'm wagering that you are feeling both excited and a touch overwhelmed at the prospect of finally getting what you want out of life. I want to reassure you that this book is all about simplicity. Each principle, exercise, hack, and story is designed to be actionable, to help you in the here and now. I want you to dive right in, let it get messy, let it ruffle your feathers. I promise you, in minutes you will begin to feel substantive, positive changes and shifts in your body and mind.

Get ready to expand your life!

A Return to Our Pure State

I have a theory: the popularity of television shows like *Survivor*, *Game of Thrones*, *American Ninja Warrior*, and *Naked and Afraid*, and our fascination with tattoos, ear stretching, statement necklaces, and fashion-forward tribal designs point to a kind of cultural yearning for rawness, for a time when, as early humans, our only goals were survival and procreation, and we enjoyed only sunlight and firelight.

The conscious self is our awareness, that part of our mind that is connected to our prefrontal cortex (the newer part of the brain that has evolved over time). This necessary and more complex part of our brain is what enables us to solve complicated social problems, manage relationships, and plan for our future—all through higher-level cognitive processes.

But that's not who we are in our pure state. Our core self, that feeling self, is our subconscious. The subconscious is tied to the more primal aspects of the brain, the amygdala and the rest of the limbic system. This is the part of our self that tethers and secures us. It's the person we were born to be, and the person we were before we grew up: our inner eight-year-old.

As we grow older, we naturally silence this part of ourselves. We have to become mature participants in the activities of the world—school, work, relationships, marriages, child-rearing, divorces. We're conditioned to follow society's rules. As we engage in the complexities of the world, the subconscious becomes quieter and the conscious becomes noisier, telling us what we should do, should say, should feel. The trouble is, these directions are often not really good for us. The Critical Thinker works too hard and is no longer in sync with the truth-telling subconscious.

As adults, we begin to live day in and day out without a moment's reflection on who we really are at the level of our soul. We are like kelp in the ocean current, swaying the way of the strongest tide. We live in a world where we are increasingly disconnected—from one another, from our desires, from our truths—because of this imbalance between our subconscious and our conscious mind.

Technology has given us access to a much wider experiential world, affording us so much in terms of interconnectivity and instant knowledge. But many of these technological advances have reinforced the lopsided relationship between our subconscious and our conscious mind. Tech, as brilliant as it is, has created a kind of interference in our ability to experience our natural world—the sea, the stars, the darkness of night. We can get stuck in the blue, sickly glow of LEDs. As a result, we have become separated from our "motherboard," our mental home base, the subconscious.

And if we let it, almost every action, function, and decision can be monitored by an appliance, computer, or other application, and all this outer surveillance can cause stress on our brains and bodies and the surrounding natural world, reinforcing a pervasive feeling of disconnection. Exposure to our beloved cell phones has been shown in some studies to have detrimental effects on our attention spans; social media divides our attention and, despite its intent to keep us connected, often undermines our sense of trust in our relationships with others.

By activating your subconscious, you can reconnect to your intuition and now hear these two parts of yourself—the instinctual, raw self, untarnished by the needs and expectations of others, *and* the critical adult who is able to distinguish between what's real and what's not, what's rational and irrational, and what's truly good for you. Once in alignment, you're more able to see, hear, and feel the energy of the SoulSpirit.

Whatever your dreams, when you open yourself up to the power of your subconscious, you will unleash a tremendous capacity to chart your own trajectory and create dominion over your life. And when you bring the energy of these three forces—the subconscious, the conscious mind, and the SoulSpirit—together, you realize that you are your own creator, moving daily toward mastery.

The program in this book will enable you to let go of any preconceptions about what you can and cannot do. You'll access your birthright, discover that anything and everything is possible. When I say "anything and everything," I mean it—some of these gifts will be beyond your current comprehension. For years we've heard about the law of attraction, and how we can attract what we want in life by believing it will be so. But imagine channeling what life wants for *you*. I hear time and time again from the celebrities, elite performers, and other high achievers with whom I work that their successes are beyond their wildest dreams. They'll detail how their dreams, as dynamic as they seemed at the time, fell short of the success they actually achieved.

You might wonder how this is possible, if what you dream is what you create.

It's possible because you are divine, whether you are aware of it or not, whether you are spiritual or not, a visionary or not. Your divinity is your birthright, and so is your success. When you limit your successes, whatever they are, to your vision and only your vision, you are limiting your outcome. When you tap into the power of the subconscious, the universe is invited in to play, to show up, to reveal its plan, to participate. You are creating a seat at the table for another entity, the ultimate fan who has more in store for you than humanly imaginable. Some people imagine this place as sitting close to God, or in whatever form divinity takes for you. Others conceive of this place of boundless opportunity and freedom as akin to the vastness of nature—the sea or the sky, the planets and the constellations. Still others evoke a deeply intimate place within themselves where it's so quiet, their thoughts are loud. What is your vision?

Chapter 2

Principle One: Come into Accountability

"You are responsible for your own life. You can't keep blaming somebody else for your dysfunction. Life is really about moving on."

—OPRAH WINFREY

Jacqui was always behind in her mortgage payments; she still owed college debts from twenty years earlier; and she juggled at least ten credit cards, keeping at least half maxed out. She owed thousands to the IRS. What does Jacqui do for a living? She's a successful television director who has won numerous awards and is known the world over for her work. She earns almost a million dollars a year. And yet she was stuck in a cycle of debt.

When she showed up in my office, all I could see was the cloud of shame that enveloped her. "I'm so embarrassed," she told me. "I don't know why I'm still in debt. I have nothing to show for all my hard work."

Indeed, she did have something to show: her problems with money.

No amount of traditional therapy had been able to help Jacqui change her habits of overspending. No amount of analysis led her to insight that undid her long history of buying beyond her means. She found herself on a perpetual cycle of working harder to only just stay out of the debt collector's reach.

My work with Jacqui entailed a huge shift in her mind-set. I didn't want her to feel shame or embarrassment. I knew the only way out of the mess she had created for herself was to make her accountable for how she fed this self-sabotaging cycle. She used the Six Principles to become aware of how she was causing the debt, and learned to take steps to truly embrace the value she created at her work. Instead of throwing money away on meaningless things, she took ownership of her hard-earned dollars and grew real assets. And it all started to change when she became accountable for herself and her behaviors.

Becoming Accountable

Becoming accountable for who you are and what you want in this life is inherently selfish. I don't mean selfish as in at someone else's expense—I mean selfish as in self-first. Living a full and happy life depends on you making that kind of commitment to yourself: to put yourself first, to honor yourself and your right to happiness, and to fill yourself up with all that the universe has to offer.

What does that entail? Becoming accountable means you will notice how you speak and act and relate to others. You will take stock of your language and how it reveals your beliefs about yourself and your own capabilities. Becoming accountable also asks that you consider your relationship with your body and health. Why? Because our bodies are vessels of energy transport. As you begin to communicate with both your subconscious and the universal energy of the SoulSpirit, the healthier, cleaner, and stronger your body (your vessel), the more powerful the energy that will emerge.

We are all aware that physical issues often point to emotional blockages; indeed, all mind-body medicine is based upon this connection between our emotions and our physical health. Practitioners such as Deepak Chopra and Louise Hay have published widely on this topic, showing their millions of readers how we can help support our wellness and avoid disease when we invest in our emotional health. In this chapter, we're going to look at what's underneath these conditions and determine how they originate. As you will see, I ask you to consider your relationship with your physical body throughout the process, so that you offer yourself the best possible opportunity for true transformation.

We live in a culture that is overly attuned to pseudo-accountability and "owning" it. In a cycle of apologies, we seem to bounce between two extremes—helping people stop playing the victim on one extreme, and on the other, demanding that they own all their problems. I find that the truth often lies in the middle. I'm presenting a different framework for understanding accountability. When I speak about becoming accountable, I am referring to a kind of self-awareness that has no bearing on others; it's just about you and your relationship with yourself. Can you be honest with yourself—about your wants and desires, your pains and worries, your needs and vulnerabilities? This is not about asking you to reveal yourself to others—this is about revealing yourself to you.

Remember my story about my relationship with John, and how he described me as controlling? At the time, I was horrified. I was also embarrassed and defensive, all at once. But my emotional reactions— as contradictory as they might seem—actually pointed to the truth of the matter. I had been acting controlling. I was continually "going General" because I thought I had to. It was all I knew. When I saw my behavior for what it was, I was able to step back and really take responsibility for my actions. I had to neutralize the General. That's an example of me becoming accountable.

This is why both becoming aware of yourself and coming into accountability can often be tricky business. With all good intentions, we can fall into patterns of behaving, thinking, and feeling that stand in opposition to what we really want. Getting at this dissonance, at the contradictions between what we truly desire and how we act, is one of the core principles of accessing the subconscious.

For example, when I first began working with Hillary, she felt overwhelmed by life. Her marriage to an emotionally abusive husband had frayed every nerve and her health was deteriorating, yet she wouldn't leave the marriage. She insisted on trying to change him and his behaviors. She was not yet able to see the abuse she seemed to be inflicting on herself by staying in the marriage. Her fear of change reinforced her comfort with the status quo, despite it hurting her. Through our work together, she discovered how removed she was from her subconscious. She had to acknowledge her part in accepting the cycle of abuse perpetuated by her husband. I said to her, "You're here for you, not your husband. You can't fix him. You are responsible for yourself."

For Hillary to come into accountability, she had to explore some provocative questions and examine her internal representations: the language we use that reinforces our false beliefs about ourselves (see "Where Are You Now?" on page 29). She finally became aware that by staying in the marriage, she made the impact of her husband's abuse even worse. In order to release herself from the role of victim and summon the strength to leave the relationship, Hillary had to stop thinking about her husband and truly put herself first.

Jacqui went through a similar set of exercises that enabled her to understand how her early childhood deprivations had morphed into the need to spend more money than she had. Her mom had raised her and her brother as a single parent, working two jobs, and Jacqui had always held on to that younger version of herself who "never had enough." She had to let go of that fearful memory so that she could fully own the successful, abundant adult she'd become. After these shifts in mind-set, she could set up practical steps to get herself out of debt and in control of her finances for good. I call this poverty consciousness, and I see it a lot in elderly people who grew up during the Depression, for example. Today, thanks to letting go of her unhealthy cycle of spending, Jacqui is happy living within her means and is able to be more successful at work.

You, too, will come to see whether the thoughts and belief systems that drive your decisions are aligned with and supportive of what you want, who you want to be, and how you can achieve those goals. Becoming aware of your thoughts, beliefs, and patterns of behavior, and acknowledging who you've become and what you really want is all part of the process of coming into accountability.

This shift doesn't have to be long and drawn out; in fact, you can achieve it through three specific exercises. Chances are if you are engaging in negative self-talk, you may be repeating negativity you heard growing up, even though you are not consciously aware of this destructive habit.

Where Are You Now?

The following questions will reveal any issues or lingering feelings that might need to be released from your mind, body, and spirit. If any one of the following conditions seems familiar, pay close attention to the ultimate take-away in Principle One to clear the way to your own truth. Asking yourself these questions will

help you get started so that you can become fully accountable to
yourself.

1. Do you find that at times you have not been operating
   from integrity? You might feel dishonest, or that you've
   taken advantage during an exchange with someone else.
2. Do you fear that you won't fit in? You might be
   avoiding social gatherings or being hypervigilant
   about your looks or behaviors.
3. Are you unsure whether others are being honest with
   you? Do you find yourself in conflict with others after
   an exchange or conversation?
4. Are you a people-pleaser? Do you put your needs aside
   for the needs of others?
5. Do you prefer to avoid honest or hard conversations?
   Do you find yourself avoiding difficult or awkward
   situations?
6. Do you feel that frankness is off putting? You might
   have become conditioned to superficial conversations,
   avoiding directness.
7. Do you get enjoyment by playing emotional or mind
   games at the expense of others?
8. Do you harbor the fear that the true you is unlikable?
   You might isolate yourself and put on pretenses when
   engaging.

If you responded "yes" to more than one of these questions,
then you will benefit from the Hypnotic Hacks (page 31).

Hypnotic Hack: Conscious Awareness

This is one of my favorite Hypnotic Hacks because it can help you quickly become more aware of the attitudes and false beliefs that might be limiting you now and in the past, and help you reorient yourself toward your subconscious and the truth of who you are. This exercise, based on neuro-linguistic programming (NLP), will help you become aware of how you regularly use language in a way that creates or reinforces negative ideas you have about yourself and your capacity for success. Try the following.

1. Think about the sayings you use on a regular basis and how they are often steeped in negativity:

   "I was blindsided."

   "It would be the death of me."

   "Over my dead body."

   "Give me a break."

   "This is killing me."

   "I would die if that happened."

   "That's so sick!"

   "I worked until I was blue in the face."

   "Just my luck."

   "Stupid me, I'm an idiot."

   "I'm a wreck."

   "I'm a hot mess."

   Even sayings that are meant for love or as a joke, such as "My heart aches for you," or "You crack me up," or "I'm dying to see you," can have a deleterious effect on how you think about yourself. Now quickly jot down all the negative sayings and phrases that you use habitually. You probably don't realize you use negative phrases and how often you do so. This exercise will help you cultivate a new awareness, so that you are more attuned to these phrases and how you use them. It's time to swap out lazy, demeaning language with phrases of authentic, positive meaning. Your subconscious finds peace in repetition, so this exercise can be done as frequently as needed.

2. Broaden the list to include any negative slogans and sayings that you hear others say—within earshot counts. If your subconscious hears it, you will react.

3. Think about your own body and how any health issues you are dealing with might be reinforced by your use of negative phrases, such as "I got tripped up," "I'm a knucklehead," "What a pain in the neck," and "That's so nerve-racking." Also, "It's a no-brainer," "I choked," "My head is splitting," and "That burns me up."

Language is powerful. Consider how using these phrases in your daily vernacular can create vulnerabilities to health issues, accidents, or other unwanted events. Look at the contrast between the phrases below:

Instead of saying,

"I was shocked" . . . say, "I was amazed."

"That's so weird" . . . say, "That's so interesting."

"I was blindsided" . . . say, "I was surprised."

"It's going to be so hard" . . . say, "It's a challenge to overcome."

"One of the pitfalls" . . . say, "One of the opportunities for growth . . ."

This exercise is very effective for coming into accountability, helping bring forth awareness of the power of our words.

Un-Causing Events

Coming into accountability does not mean you have to atone for all you've done in the past. It doesn't mean writing a letter of apology—we'd all have novels. Instead, it means that you adopt a mind-set of honesty. For example, all of us can be late for many reasons. Mostly we are late because we left the house, office, or wherever . . . late. How refreshing to tell your host the truth: "I'm so sorry I'm late, I *left* the house late." It's honest and charming—rather than creating a lie about the traffic or the dog. Lies are never worth the lie. You're lying because you think it will make the other person feel better, but the lies just make another person feel worse, and no one really believes you anyway. The charade of the lie just makes the situation worse. Why are lies so corrosive? Lies and excuses separate us from our subconscious and one another. Excuses carry energy just like the truth does. And we all know the freedom of truth just feels better.

With this new awareness of your own internal representations, try to create some change in how you experience yourself with others. In some ways, you can think of this exercise as an act of forgiveness or compassion. You can also think of it as simply a way to move out of a negative perception of an experience with someone else and let it go so that it does not hold *you* back.

Just for kicks and giggles, bring to mind a situation in which you felt hurt by a friend, family member, colleague, or former lover. We can all bring at least one instance to mind, I am sure. We have all felt hurt—intentionally or not—by other people. But do we want this hurt to stick to us, or do we want to leverage it and extend the learnings?

Kyle came to me because he felt his rage was out of control. He'd recently been given a warning at work because of his outbursts with colleagues. He also admitted to me that he'd been in a fender bender because of road rage. Anger, I explained, is often a defense for a perceived injury, leaving people feeling stuck in victimhood.

"I really don't have any control anymore," he admitted to me sheepishly. Under hypnosis, I had him replay a couple of recent events when he had felt intense anger. As he brought these incidents to mind, I then asked him how he had contributed to each circumstance.

Kyle recalled an instance when he was in the middle of a custody battle with his soon-to-be ex-wife. He was speaking to his lawyer while driving, and got triggered by any little thing that happened on the road. Did that guy cut him off? Was that woman slowing down in the left lane? He was numb to his own subconscious, unable to separate from the screaming thrall of his conscious mind that was so angry and upset over the custody battle.

As you will see in the exercise on page 35, a key to coming into accountability is truly understanding how you contribute to the emotional events that occur in your life.

Whether a hurt done to us is real or imagined almost doesn't matter—the subconscious takes it in. In order to un-cause negative or difficult events, we need to first extend the olive branch to ourselves— forgive ourselves and accept that we are all doing the best we can. In this exercise, you will come to understand how you contribute to what happens to or around you.

I call this exercise "This Was Me." This exercise enables you to reset your point of view so you stop seeing yourself as a passive player reacting to a situation that you had no control over and instead recognize the role you played in what happened. You can release your negative feelings about yourself and speak from a place of forgiveness, so that the subconscious can come forth. Resolution emerges from this kind of accountability. When you ask yourself how your actions helped to create a certain situation (rather than waiting for an effect to occur), you can direct your experience and its outcome. Sometimes this shift requires building, and sometimes it requires deconstruction. If you're in a place where you've caused problems for yourself in the past, it can help you un-cause them in the future.

Hypnotic Hack: This Was Me

In order to come into accountability (for any situation, from a minor distraction to a major hurdle in your life, regardless of how big or small), try the following:

1. Close your eyes and go within.
2. Think of a time and place where you experienced a negative event.
3. Mentally survey the way you feel as the event replays in your mind. What do you see, hear, smell, taste, and feel?
4. Now ask yourself *how you caused* this event to occur. What did you do to allow this situation to happen or to create it? How did you participate or fuel the situation?
5. Stay open to the flood of denial that initially rushes your senses. This uncomfortable feeling is your defensiveness releasing.
6. Now ask yourself *why you caused* this event to occur, allowing yourself time to process the answers coming to you.
7. Now imagine a time in the future when you would choose to *not* cause the event.

Transposing Hurt and Resentment

Our lives are inevitably entangled with others. There's no getting around this fact. So while we are here on this earth, we can benefit from staying flexible in our minds when we are impacted by the actions, words, or behaviors of others. This means learning how to release ourselves from hurt, disappointment, anger, and other negative emotions we experience in response to others. For example, you might have been excluded from a guest list for a neighbor's wedding; friends of yours were invited, and you feel hurt and angry and embarrassed. Or perhaps your boss gave you some honest feedback at work; you know it's true, but why did he have to be so critical?

Releasing the hurt, anger, or resentment toward others frees you from the confines that can keep you separate from your subconscious. This next exercise enables you to transpose these feelings and activate your ability to soften in order to ease old or stubborn hurts and reinforce your connection to your subconscious. In hypnosis, this is a powerful form of release and helps open you further to your subconscious.

Hypnotic Hack: Transposition

. . . .

This hack activates the three positions that enable you to let go of resentment or bitterness or anger toward another person. You will be asked to consider three different points of view, including your point of view; the other person's perspective; and the third, the so-called "God" position, which represents a higher or more omniscient view of the encounter. In order to resolve any given disagreement or negative encounter, it's important that you activate both the other person's viewpoint and the omniscient, objective view so that your own perspective can soften and shift away from the negative into a more positive light.

1. Close your eyes and go within.

2. Bring to mind the contentious encounter. You are looking from your own perspective, through your own eyes.

3. Identify, feel, and sit with all the emotions that are present.

4. Now imagine the same encounter from the other person's perspective, looking through their eyes back at you.

5. Notice and feel all the emotions the other person must be experiencing in response to you.

6. Allow this new perspective on the event to evolve.

7. Now imagine yourself high up on a platform, centered high above the two of you, looking down on the event. What do you see? What do you hear? How do you feel *about both participants* in this situation? Notice how much more informed you are from this position.

8. Recognize and feel the truth of all three perspectives. Acknowledge the feeling of freedom in this neutral point of view. Welcome this new awareness and the options of neutrality.

Any time you release your position on a matter, you open yourself up to another perspective. Physically imagining yourself in motion, adopting other points of view or ways of thinking about a situation, brings in your subconscious, which can see an event from all sides.

Have fun with this one, use it often and enjoy the view!

Call Upon SoulSpirit

Trying anything for the first time can trigger a fight-or-flight-
or-freeze response. Don't shy away from these feelings. Sit with
them. Let them run through you. Try not to evaluate or analyze
them. Remind yourself that you are not alone. The world is bigger
than you, and trusting in your connection to the wider universe
can be a source of comfort and direction. Right now, send out a
call to your SoulSpirit. Say a prayer. Meditate. Observe something
beautiful. Shift your gaze toward the sky. Connect.

The Power Position of Openness

Coming into accountability is a constant in our lives. Just like breathing, eating, and sleeping, it's a powerful way to clean your slate with
yourself and the universe so that you can connect with your subconscious.

As you proceed with the principles, stay flexible and open. Know
that you will indeed return to this lesson to stay honest and clear about
who you are and where you are at any given juncture of your life. And
of course, whenever you feel the need, call upon the SoulSpirit to
guide you.

Chapter 3

Principle Two: Tap into
Your Subconscious Power

"Every piece of technology, every piece of art, basically everything manmade comes from an idea."

—PHARRELL WILLIAMS

Picture a woman who has pretty much everything she could desire—
fortune, beauty, wisdom. She had gathered her tribe of like-minded
women to celebrate a milestone birthday to which I was invited. I love
giving gifts and spoiling my friends, but at first, I was not at all sure
what to give someone who—on the surface—seemed to want for nothing. After much thought, I decided that the *something* she might value
most was actually an *experience*. I would give her what fortune and
well-intentioned friends could not give her; I would give her *magic*.

That evening, we ate, we drank, we talked—we celebrated and
cheered on our friend. It was late by the time coffee was served and all
the gifts were opened—except for mine. I had waited until the end. I
was a bit nervous, because this group of mostly new acquaintances was
a tough crowd, a seasoned bunch, a room full of trailblazing women
who had pretty much seen it all. Being a trendsetter myself, I pushed
through my jitters and forged ahead with my plan, as I had many times
before.

I took out my large signature bag from under my chair and began handing out twenty-five colorful, light-up tutus. Yes—tutus! I had scoured the internet in search of these wondrous, girlish testaments to fun parties and endless youth, and brought layers and layers of pink, green, and yellow tulle stacked high in delicious airy piles. These reminders of sleepovers, dressing up, and discovering lip gloss, all long before thoughts of growing up entered our imaginations. That magical time when you squealed and giggled without any self-consciousness. In other words, when we are young, we are more naturally tied to our subconscious.

I instructed everyone to put their tutus on over their lady clothes, find the hidden LED pocket, and light them up. All at once, the nervous giggles turned to laughter. And before I knew it, two dozen grown women were out of their seats and moving around looking at one another in absolute delight.

But I wasn't done with my bag of surprises.

Next, I handed out small gold pouches and declared, "This moment is dedicated to our birthday girl. May she continue to shine bright like all of us are doing now. May we all find our inner eight-year-olds, that part of ourselves that is not afraid to put on their tutus and dance with abandon! Let's all agree that no matter why we put our tutus away long ago, deep in a drawer or tucked away in a box and long lost—be it sickness, divorce, abuse by another or ourselves—we have now found our tutus again."

Each woman opened her tiny gold pouch to find a fistful of glitter— and all together we raised our hands in unison, filling the air around us with girlhood *magic*. I explained that this reconnection to ourselves continues whether it's next week or next month. "You will inevitably find glitter on your body or clothes to remind you of this night. Your inner eight-year-old will relish the remembrance of a magical night and your inner softness that remains with you always. The glitter will be a reminder of tonight, our beautiful friend, and of your connecting once again with you inner, softer spirit."

I have many photos of that night. In them, you can see the bright, shining faces, laughter, giggles, and celebration. But in one corner of the photos, one woman is hanging back, holding her tutu in one hand, unable to put it on. I remembered her. That night, I approached her, asking if she was all right.

She said, "I never had one of these. I was not a girly girl."

"Neither was I," I assured her. "I wore cowboy boots and rode horses. I was dusty and sweaty and was not wearing tutus. Tonight isn't about the tutus—it's about having fun."

This woman is an accomplished physician and serious-minded in her career; I knew she was having trouble opening herself into the energy of the evening. She was not just resisting putting on the tutu; she was resisting joining the party, and participating, and playing, because she was self-conscious, held back by her Critical Thinker.

I could tell that no amount of my urging was going to convince her to join the rest of us, though I did share one more thought.

"Tutu, Tonka truck, baseball mitt, or skateboard, these relics from our childhood are symbols that connect us to our purity." I wanted her subconscious to hear that message.

So regardless of our plaything of choice, all of us associate these vestiges of our youth with an inner part of ourselves; the object becomes not a relic but a symbolic embodiment of the inner eight-year-old, a physical stand-in for your playfulness that gives you direct access to your subconscious. This younger self is never caustic or cynical. Instead, this unfettered self is the primal, younger you who embraces the joy, the love, the play, the mysteries of life. She or he comes from a position of no agenda or strategy, but loves symbolism in any form, stretching way beyond gender and other categories that try to define and limit us.

This tutu story, along with many others, has come to embody both the capacity we all have for this playfulness of the inner eight-year-old, as well as how the Critical Thinker can sometimes try to pull rank, keeping us separate and away from the party of life. And yet our culture often resists the battle cry of the inner eight-year-old, relying on the more rational, thoughtful behavior of the Critical Thinker. Think of the magical tutus Serena Williams is known for donning on the tennis court and her childlike twirls after she wins.

Living in Trance

As we've seen in the previous chapters, living in trance and staying connected to our subconscious is hampered by the world we live in today. Its complexity, its nonstop pace, its reduced access to the untouched natural world, and, yes, even the interference of technology. And yet we can reconnect with our internal motherboard. Our biggest obstacle is not outside us but inside us: we simply forget how to use the subconscious and its power. In this chapter, you will return to this natural state, the land of the tutu, the Tonka truck, the scooter, and the toy train. You will find your very own path, and it will not be hard—it will be easy.

Why is connecting to the inner eight-year-old so important? Because this is the adult way of living in trance. From a hypnotherapy perspective, relaxing into trance or achieving "trance state" enables people to be completely relaxed with access to their subconscious. The magic, the creative state, the genius. A bigger, broader perspective of your life and your potential self. The nothingness of trance allows everything to appear: solutions, formulations, calculations, creations, ingenuity, where deliciousness lives. Tapping into trance is a sort of guided daydreaming.

Children know this state well. They become so absorbed in play, they lose their sense of where they are. They are immersed completely in an experience, a degree of engagement that has been studied by scientists and described as the state of "flow." Indeed, pioneering psychologist Mihaly Csikszentmihalyi coined the term "flow state," based upon the experiences of elite athletes, artists, musicians, scientists, yoginis, and others who can become so immersed in their own process that they lose an awareness of the critical world and instead are completely absorbed in a pleasurable activity. This kind of deep engagement is a characteristic of play—something eight-year-old children specialize in!

But experiencing flow is not reserved for the few outliers among us; indeed, it's accessible by any one of us if we are open and connected to the subconscious, the other part of our mind. Imagine you are walking alone through a big, wide-open field. You are looking down at your feet and the path before you, somewhat aware of the noises around you—birds, insects, perhaps the wind as it rustles through the leaves on nearby trees. You catch the scent of nearby plants, which has a tangy minty-ness to it. All your senses are pulsing as they take in the energy and information the environment is transmitting. As you continue walking, it's as if you enter your surroundings; instead of observing or simply sensing the natural world, *you are immersed in it.* You sense the air moving, you imagine the deer in the woods, you can feel the scurrying of the rabbits. If someone were to ask you to create a picture, you believe you could bring this entire visceral scene to life. But if you were to photograph your experience, it would contain none of the details you were sensing.

Being in trance and accessing your subconscious is similar to this immersion in nature when the visceral intensity of the senses can trigger an experience of flow. When you connect to your subconscious, you wake up your senses and turn down the volume of your Critical Thinker so it cannot impose its worries or concerns. You give your inner eight-year-old permission to show up for you. We all have this choice, this potential to connect to this inner resource that lives within us. Your subconscious is unique to you, just like your fingerprints. And what your subconscious will tell you will be uniquely true for you. Indeed, that's a phrase I use all the time with my clients, especially when they are wondering if what they are feeling is right or okay. I tell them, "If you feel it, it's true for you."

I have a question for you: Can you, for a moment, let yourself open up to the possibility that this part of yourself is alive and well and ready to be explored?

Where Are You Now?

How tuned into your subconscious are you? Do you wake up at 3:00 or 4:00 a.m.? Do you find yourself envying other people? Their houses, cars, partners, status? When you are at a social event or party, do you notice that you are not having fun? Have you been to the doctor and received a surprising diagnosis? Do people often tell you that you look tired?

Before jumping to any conclusions, let's take a moment to consider what's inside these questions, keeping in mind that this process is not about trying to make you feel "less than." In fact, it's all about letting your subconscious reveal your true self, your true feelings, and what you need to be most happy. However, as you begin to access your subconscious, you may experience some discomfort. Don't judge these feelings. Simply stay open and alert to all the thoughts and feelings that shake loose. And pay attention to any signs of the trapped energy coming unbound.

Please respond to the following questions as a way to gauge your current connection to your subconscious.

1. Do you check your smartphone constantly, looking for new texts, tweets, or posts?
2. Do you frequently find yourself searching for something to wear?
3. Are you usually late to meetings, events, or appointments?
4. Do your emotions or feelings often change throughout the day?
5. Is change difficult for you? Do you tend to react strongly to changes in schedules or moves of any sort?
6. Do you often find yourself angry or sad?
7. Do you often feel depleted or depressed?
8. Are you often restless or anxious?

If you responded "yes" to more than three of these questions, then it's possible that either you're not currently tapped into your subconscious or that your subconscious and your conscious mind are out of sync with each other. Any one of these conditions or behaviors can point to a need for you to turn up the volume of your subconscious and turn down the volume of your conscious mind.

How False Beliefs Keep Our Subconscious
and Our Conscious Mind Out of Sync

We all have those times when we wake up at 3:00 or 4:00 a.m. in the morning for seemingly no reason. Typically, these are periods of our lives when we have a lot going on or are in the midst of change. During these times of transition, your subconscious literally wakes you up, reminding you, *Let me give you more hours of waking time to solve your problems, weather the storm, or figure out a solution to an issue.* When you wake up, it's simply a signal from your subconscious that you need more daytime to problem-solve.

One of the ways the subconscious works for you is by helping you identify false beliefs that keep you from yourself and the source of its wisdom and energy. A false belief is any idea or conception of yourself that is not true. Because it's untrue, it limits you and holds you back from fulfilling your potential. False beliefs manifest in our behaviors and show up in our daily lives. For example, false beliefs about the self might be "I am an ineffectual person" or "I am a troubled person" or "I am a weak person." If you believe yourself to be ineffectual, you will feel that you can never get anything done. If you think of yourself as a troubled person, you will believe that you will always have problems in life. If you think of yourself as a weak person, you will feel afraid of change and challenges.

False beliefs show up in how we confront situations, relationships, and most of all in our inner dialogue with ourselves. Most of the time, these false narratives stem from a sense of lack and a separation from both our subconscious and the SoulSpirit. We will dive into the various forms of drought in chapter 9; for now, I want you to become aware of any beliefs about yourself that are negative. One of the many beautiful qualities of the subconscious is how it can easily root out false beliefs so they no longer sabotage our ability to play big in our lives. As soon as you identify beliefs about yourself that are untrue, you can use your subconscious to uproot them.

Before doing the following exercise, make a list of your false beliefs and set it aside.

Rid Yourself of False Beliefs

1. Close your eyes and go within.
2. Bring to mind one of the false beliefs you put on your list.
3. Imagine this belief written on a blackboard.
4. Now imagine walking to the blackboard and erasing it.
5. Create an affirmation that is the opposite of the false belief. (For example, if you wrote, "I am unloved," now say aloud, "I am loved.")
6. Call upon the SoulSpirit, bringing to mind whatever form of divinity makes most sense to you. Say to the SoulSpirit, "I know I am loved."

This exercise may seem simplistic, and it is. It may even seem a bit hokey—I get it. But false beliefs are just a mirage. When you get close to them, they disappear. They vaporize when addressed and are easy to dispel once you see and acknowledge their untruth.

Keeping our conscious and subconscious in sync and in balance means the conscious is not overwanting, overextending, overcontrolling. When it's connected to the subconscious, it calms down, enables you to feel grounded and tempered, and gives you a sense of fullness and *satiety*.

Hypnotic Hack: Cancel, Cancel!

This is a classic hypnotherapy exercise that I learned in my hypnotherapy training (see Hypnotic Hack: Conscious Awareness on page 31). Like an eight-year-old, your subconscious hears everything and believes it's true. So you want to be mindful of what you say and what you listen to, given that he or she's listening. If, in passing, you say something like, "If I don't get that job, I'm going to die!" your inner child will take in that fear of violence and death.

To protect yourself from this harmful energy when these sayings roll out of your mouth (and most of us do say them, often without thinking about it), simply follow up by saying to yourself, *"Cancel, cancel."*

Try it—you'll find that words are powerful when it comes to the fragile children inside of us. This hack is very helpful when you're just starting to be more mindful about the role of language in the subconscious. Ultimately, the goal is to change your vernacular to supportive statements, such as, "If that job is mine, I will get it."

You can use this hack throughout the process of tapping into your subconscious and learning how to play big. It can help you release internal representations, false beliefs, patterns of behaviors, and mistaken judgments (you will read about these in chapters 4 and 5).

The Stickiness of Separation

Being separate from our subconscious has a cascading effect on our lives. When we are not plugged into our subconscious, our conscious mind becomes overpowered, and we experience others as sources of comparison—in a negative way. On the other hand, when our subconscious and our conscious mind are in sync, then the lives of others— what they have, what they accomplish—do not trigger jealousy or envy, but inspire joy and support.

Additionally, when you are out of balance, you are likely to perceive that what is good for others is bad for you. When you are in balance, you are likely to perceive that what is good for others is good for you, too. The truth is, whatever is in another person's bucket—a promotion, a new husband or wife, bountiful fertility—has little to do with you but everything to do with the happiness around you!

When you are connected to your subconscious, you are more likely to trust that what's good for one of us is good for all of us. This collective reciprocity is evident when individuals, communities, and even countries come together to participate in humanitarian causes. Think of how the world at large responded to the tsunami in Phuket, Thailand; Hurricane Katrina; and even the ongoing crisis in the Middle East. When one community is affected by catastrophe, people come together globally to help. It's human nature to want to help those who are less fortunate or whose lives have been imperiled by conflict, drought, or other calamities.

This same dynamic occurs in times of celebration as well—when the Berlin Wall came down (I happened to be in Berlin as the wall came down!), when a newborn panda arrives, or when France won the FIFA World Cup. The celebrations happen on a global stage, spreading joy the world over. As the aphorism made famous by John F. Kennedy goes, "A rising tide lifts all boats." In other words, a tide does not just lift one boat—it lifts all boats.

Another sign of being separated from your subconscious is that you get stuck in forethought. I have a vivid memory of a lovely dinner party I attended when I was still with John. The people were interesting, the food sublime. The décor of the home was sumptuous. And yet I found myself sitting among my peers feeling as if I were alone. I watched the camaraderie and cheer around me, unable to feel the fun myself. In hindsight, I now see that I was experiencing a profound sense of separation—not only from the party, but from myself. I was an observer, not a participant.

This kind of inability to experience pleasure is a hallmark of an ignored or blocked subconscious. The feeling of disconnection can ultimately have devastating effects. It did for me—when I finally left John, for instance, I became somewhat reclusive for a while. Part of this retreat was healing, and I needed the alone time to reconnect with myself. But after a few months, I knew that my social disconnection was hampering my wellness. By that time, I had become more tuned into my subconscious, and it was that soft, playful, fun voice that urged me to jump back into the world around me.

Do you see the pattern here? The thread of connection back to others is the connection back to your subconscious.

Here's another example of the kind of emotional entrapment that comes from separation: You're on vacation with your partner or family or friends. Everyone is in good spirits, but you (or someone else) keeps worrying. When someone suggests a boat outing, Doug or Debi Downer reminds you of all that could go wrong—sudden inclement weather, someone falling overboard—you name it. Then, when someone else suggests going out for fish or sushi, Doug or Debi pipes up with, "Can't you get sick from eating raw fish?"

This kind of habit of mind brought one of my clients, Maria, in to see me. A former executive, she'd been a stay-at-home mom to her two sons, now ages five and seven, since her first son was born. She said that she was happy not working and being able to focus on her children and her marriage, but she always felt "disconnected."

I asked her to elaborate.

Maria described feeling "like an outcast" and unable to connect with the other moms. "I'm always just thinking about how I'm different and what I should/could/would be doing with my time instead of having playdates with my kids."

When I asked her if she enjoyed herself at all, she said, "Not really—I feel like I'm always thinking about what's next. I'm never in the moment."

This kind of negative observation or observing forethought is a practice, a habit, and an indication that the person cannot get out of the way of an otherwise beautiful moment. He or she gets *stuck in forethought* of what could be.

Underneath the states of both envy and being stuck in forethought is the false belief that you are lacking in some way. In Maria's case, she needed to ground herself more fully in what mattered to her; she needed to feel that her choices—staying at home with her sons, for example—were aligned with what she wanted. The more aware she was of her own choices, the more she could stop short-circuiting her own experience. Planning ahead is a great thing, but too much planning can mute the subconscious and its power to keep you spontaneous and in the moment.

Sometimes when you feel outside of your own experience, separate from others in some way because of another change in your life, it's even more important to tune into your subconscious. This is the exercise I used with Maria, to help her understand that her choice to stay home, in her case, was indeed working for her. Once she felt connected to her true, inner self, she no longer felt so separate from those around her. You can also use this to reconnect to your subconscious for any reason—when you're too focused on others, when you feel like you can't join the party, or when you're in retreat mode, withdrawing from fun social occasions.

Hypnotic Hack: Subconscious Primer
. . . .

This exercise awakens the subconscious, bringing forth the "I" that knows what is best for you. As I like to say to my clients, "You know and I know that you know." The subconscious is that part of yourself who knows better and does better. It is your higher self, your best self.

With this exercise, you are consciously asking your subconscious to come forward.

1. Close your eyes and go within.
2. Once centered, open your eyes and look in the mirror at yourself. Focus on your eyes.
3. Think these thoughts in this order, taking your time with each one:

    - I *see* who you are.
    - I *hear* who you are.
    - I *feel* who you are.
    - I *know* who you have been.
    - I *am* who you will be.
    - I *am* all things.
    - I *know* all things.
    - I *feel* all things.
    - I *am* all life.
    - I *feel* all life.
    - I *will remain* all life.

Use It Now!

Your subconscious is not meant just for the esoteric. It's eminently actionable and can work for you on a very practical level to help solve daily challenges or resolve annoyances. Have you ever misplaced something in your home, briefcase, or office? You know it's somewhere, but can't remember where you stashed it. Have you arrived at an event and spent fretful minutes searching frantically for a parking spot? Perhaps it's raining and your shoes, hair, or clothes won't survive the trek from the car. We all know these situations—not necessarily dire, but so inconvenient!

Hypnotic Hack: Finding Your Stuff

1. Close your eyes and go within.
2. Recall the last time you saw the missing item.
3. Staying relaxed, imagine reaching out to touch the item.
4. Bring to mind a pleasurable feeling associated with the item.
5. Visually replay the event where you were last in contact. Staying relaxed, imagine your surroundings, be with your thoughts.
6. Recall and connect to the flow of information that originally recorded the event. Your relaxed subconscious will lead you to the item.

This exercise is my go-to in times like these. It can be used for a myriad of purposes! Try it for that lost credit card or the next time you're searching for the perfect parking place close to the entrance door. I like to think of this hack as a road test for your subconscious, a way to prime its pump and keep it active in the busyness of daily life.

Recently, I helped my client Beverly find her pearls, which had "gone missing" from her jewelry box. She called me in desperation, as she was packing to leave her family vacation home and needed to make her flight.

"I've looked everywhere! I've got to find them!"

I knew she had hidden them so well that now she couldn't find them; you know the feeling. She was so upset at herself that her fear had turned to anger, blocking any chance of her activating her subconscious.

I first tried to help her calm down. "We'll find them," I assured her.

Then I took her through the steps above, gently suggesting that she tune into the soft, warm feeling that she associates with her precious pearls. She began to talk: "I remember thinking pearls are an organism and they can't go into a box or a safe—they need to breathe," my client described her logic.

"Then I remember thinking they should be kept somewhere soft and safe," she said, getting excited.

I reminded her to shed the desperate feeling of having lost the pearls and instead relax into the calming warmth of last holding them, so that the memory of that feeling would bring her back to the place, the reveal, the moment. With a few random outbursts of "I have a flight to catch," "I don't have time" and "I'm *not* leaving this island without my pearls!" for the most part, she held it together and returned to trance.

Sure enough, Beverly remembered that she had last worn her pearls with her favorite Missoni dress—"They matched perfectly," she exclaimed.

She then ran to her chest of drawers and found the Missoni dress carefully folded (because of its delicate knit fabric), and what was nestled in between the folds? The pearls.

Consciously, she really believed she had turned her home upside down looking for the pearls and had already searched every single drawer, but that's the trick of the overly reactive conscious mind. Logically, you *think* you've looked everywhere, but the truth is quite the opposite.

Your subconscious is a seeker, a finder, a resolver; it simply requires you to relax and play along in the spirit of can-do.

Here's another hack that can help you find something—my clients love to use this to find a parking space, for instance.

Hypnotic Hack:
Finding the Perfect Parking Space

1. Close your eyes and go within.
2. Then, with your eyes open, approach the parking lot or structure and mentally connect to your subconscious.
3. Say to your subconscious, "You know the perfect space for me. Lead me to my perfect parking space." This will align your desire (perfect space) with the universe's desire (your comfort and well-being).
4. Stay flexible so you can turn the wheel when you feel compelled to, letting the energy lead you in the right time to your perfect space.
   The gist of this hack is staying in the mind-set that life is easy and you are ready to play along. Your space awaits you!

Put on *Your* Tutu and Dance

Are you ready to open up to your own creative abundance? Are you ready to take the next step out of this place of disconnection and fragmentation by calling upon the power of your subconscious self? Are you ready to tap into your primal source of intelligence? Are you ready to uncover the potential to make your life abundantly better?

In order for this transformation to be possible, it's absolutely necessary to tap into your subconscious. Which is not to say that you are unaware of your subconscious. But in today's bustling, tech-driven life, it's often difficult to hear the whisper or attune yourself to this primal part of ourselves. Indeed, the conscious mind tends to be noisy and bossy, telling us what to do and how to do it, no matter what "it" is. Since the conscious mind is in charge of higher-order thinking—making complicated decisions, problem-solving, directing the logistics of our lives—it can easily get carried away and become too officious. That's when we need the balancing effect of our subconscious. This persona is spirited, frank, and guileless—equal parts rambunctious and wise, both vulnerable and resilient. If the subconscious stumbles, it doesn't hesitate to get up and run, without missing a beat. (In other words, the inner eight-year-old does not stop to worry about a scraped knee or to sheepishly check to see who saw the fall.)

All of us have this primal, childlike essence inside of us, and yet as we grow up, as we mature and age, we naturally grow away from this instinctual way of being. As I mentioned, when I was a child, I was always a tomboy, and no amount of parental guidance was going to change that. Pretty, frilly things were okay, but they had to be sturdy enough not to ruin my fun while horseback riding, hiking, and playing sports. Then one day we paint our nails, grow our hair, and put the magic behind us. We get practical. We have to earn a living. We grow up and become pragmatic and forward-thinking. The key is to keep our inner eight-year-old accessible in spite of our adult responsibilities.

Your inner eight-year-old can also be thought of as your intuition, that inner truth-teller. She (or he) is not afraid of telling it like it is. If you've ever been around an eight-year-old, you know you can't get anything past them; they call you on everything. Just the other day, a good friend and her daughter were visiting. The young girl, who is on the cusp of turning eight, said she was hungry and asked for a snack. I propped her up on the kitchen counter and went to get a spoonful of almond butter. I said nonchalantly, "This, my dear, is for you. It has your name written all over it."

The girl looked at the spoon from top to bottom, then looked back at me and said, "This doesn't have my name on it!"

Classic eight-year-old!

Honesty reigns above all else for your inner eight-year-old, which is why we can trust him or her; it is tied directly to our deepest, most primal survival instincts.

When we can stay tethered to this part of ourselves, we give ourselves the opportunity to live more enriching, satisfying lives. Think of your subconscious as the part of yourself that is waiting to give you everything you've ever wanted. She's symbiotic; she's a giver and a taker. She's the speaker of your soul, the connection to your playful, mystical self. If you want to come out of the shadows and claim your destiny, you will need to tap into your subconscious and the magic of your inner eight-year-old. And have I mentioned the energy and drive that come from this connection to the primal you? The fun, the pleasure, the real you! As you rediscover this youthful self, get ready to enjoy energy that focuses from floodlight to laser beam.

Hypnotic Hack: Tonkas and Tutus

The persona of our subconscious is like that of an eight-year-old; in this exercise, you can practice re-experiencing this innate, spontaneous, playful part of yourself.

1. Close your eyes and settle in.
2. Imagine a time from your childhood when you enjoyed play completely.
3. See what you saw, hear what you heard, and feel what you felt.
4. Immerse yourself fully in that experience.
5. Now hear your mother/father/guardian (or any adult authority figure) calling you away from the fun scene.
6. Notice the difference between the playful you and the now-responsible you, feeling the call of having to do something.

The moment when the responsibility of modern life steps in, the subconscious feels constrained. This is a fact of life, an inevitable part of the human condition. At the same time, we all still have access to our lost metaphorical "Tonkas and tutus"—whether that's the motorcycle in the garage, the velvet slippers in the back of the closet, or the beach house from your childhood dreams. When we form special attachments to certain "toys," they typically represent a hearkening back to our inner eight-year-old. Many times these grown-up toys (cars, planes, boats, grills, candles, warm blankets, she-sheds—the list is endless) are mere replacements for the original ones that made our hearts sing. Even our cultural obsessions with symbols—such as peace signs, Hamsa hands, evil eyes, Om, unicorns, dream catchers, fairies, and hearts—represent a symbolic connection to our subconscious. Use your own symbols to connect and remind you of who you really are—bring forward that best part of you.

Regardless of whether you put on that tutu or push that Tonka truck, know this: we all have an inner eight-year-old—she might be a tomboy, he might be a diva, she might be a glitter girl, he might be a rebel, or she might be someone in between. The point is to listen to her or him, and listen closely, so this part of yourself will emerge and remind you of who you really are. As you prepare for the next principle, it's important to keep in mind that your subconscious is not just one thing. Nor is it static. It's a fluid part of you that needs to be nurtured and fed in order to be kept alive and well.

Chapter 4

Principle Three: Move Toward or Away

"I've learned that people will forget what you said, people will forget what you did, but people will never forget how you made them feel."

—MAYA ANGELOU

Did you know that 95 percent of what we do, think, and feel occurs without our conscious control? As humans, we spend most of the day and night running on automatic pilot. And at a most basic level, that automaticity is designed to avoid what's bad for us and move us toward what is good.

However, when we are split from our subconscious, this instinctual system runs amok. Instead of moving toward what benefits us, we move away. And instead of moving away from what can harm us, we move toward people, places, and situations that undermine us. Have you ever found yourself having to purposefully curb your cyber-checking on an ex-lover? Have you felt dependent on something—particular foods, alcohol, or drugs—that interferes with you living your best life? Sometimes we find ourselves attracting what doesn't benefit us and rejecting what is good for us, and this happens when the subconscious remains buried or our subconscious and our conscious mind are out of sync.

The goal of Principle Three, "Move Toward or Away," is to pay attention to your habits of mind and behaviors so that you can become aware of patterns that may be both undermining your connection to your subconscious and creating a kind of mixed signal between your subconscious and your conscious mind. This principle is another step toward growing your subconscious power and your ability to know what's good for you . . . or not.

Moving toward or away is natural—even bacteria, the most basic form of life, move away from what they perceive as harmful stimuli. However, when we lose our connection to our subconscious power, or we let the conscious mind dominate, our movements toward or away from people, places, and situations can undermine our happiness. Fine-tuning this awareness will bring you another step closer to using the insight of your subconscious to shift into positive, expansive actions that will cascade in all areas of your life.

In this chapter, you will be seeing your patterns more clearly, bringing your subconscious and your conscious mind into closer alignment, and positioning yourself to make better, more positive decisions.

The Scientific Roots of Moving Toward or Away

Scientists, including both psychologists and neuroscientists, have described approach-avoidance behavior as an innate neural circuit built in to protect our survival. Going back as far as Charles Darwin, and including current neuroscientists such as Joseph LeDoux (author of *The Emotional Brain*, among other books), as well as Antonio Damasio (author of *Descartes' Error* and *Self Comes to Mind*, among others), describe the approach-avoidance response as automatic, because it happens underneath conscious awareness and happens almost immediately, before the conscious mind has time to perceive a person or situation as dangerous . . . or not. Just like our built-in system of fight, flight, or freeze, approach-avoidance is a rudimentary way to protect us (though we are no longer running from predators on the savannah!) and is therefore very primal and reflective of an instinctive connection between our brains and our bodies. I refer to this survival mechanism as moving toward or away—because it is an extension of the relationship between the subconscious and the conscious mind.

When we move away from danger and toward someone, somewhere, something beneficial, we are expressing two important things: a strong connection to our subconscious and a balanced relationship between the subconscious and the conscious mind. As we saw in the last chapter, when either of these becomes tenuous or out of sync, we can get stuck in undermining behaviors—we move toward what's not good for us and away from what is.

Further, since we must rely on our conscious mind to help us with higher-level thinking and more complicated decisions, we want to make sure that this connection between the subconscious and our Critical Thinker is "clean and clear," without any interference from habits that are no longer useful. What's important to understand in relation to keeping your subconscious and your conscious mind in sync is making sure you pay attention to the signals the subconscious is emitting, so that all your decisions—conscious and subconscious—are authentic and truly in your best interest.

In my practice, for instance, I help my clients realize why they tend to be attracted to certain types of people or keep finding themselves in similar types of situations. Sometimes these patterns reflect a good, solid connection between the subconscious and the conscious mind. But often clients will use the question of whether they move toward or away as a means of gaining insight into why they stay stuck in patterns of behavior that keep them unhappy. For instance, Joanna came to me frustrated and feeling hopeless. Nearing her late thirties, she wanted to settle down with a good man, she told me, and then start a family. As we began to look at what might be preventing this desire from becoming realized, it became apparent that Joanna was much more comfortable being a serial dater. She loved getting to know men, put out positive energy, and ostensibly made it clear that she wanted a "real relationship," as she said. Looking a bit closer at her history, she then began to realize that as soon as a new guy would get "close," she would back away, cancel dates, and return to online dating apps to look for someone new.

Joanna had not been aware of how she moved away from what she supposedly wanted.

Here's another example. One of my clients, Phil, took a new job in a city almost two hours from his hometown. When asked why he took the job, he said it was a "great opportunity and a chance to move up" in his company. A few months later, Phil was miserable. He spent every night down at the local pub or online looking at porn. He didn't miss his ex-wife (their split was mutual), but he missed his old life, his friends, and his extended family. Plus, he was not really enjoying work or applying himself at his new job.

What Phil did not want to admit—to me or himself—was that he took the job because he wanted to get far, far away from his ex-wife. As he and I worked on tapping into his subconscious, he realized that he was actually moving *away* from his ex, not *toward* a new job. It's not that the move was bad for Phil; it was that he didn't fully understand his motivation for moving. Next I helped Phil shift his orientation toward his new job and his new town (see the "Pivot" exercise on page 68). In a few weeks, Phil began to refocus his energy on his career and figured out ways to stay in touch with his "old peeps." He also joined a gym, where he met some new friends. With his new orientation *to-ward* this new chapter in his life (instead of *away* from his last), both the pub and the porn just fell off his obsession list, naturally and without notice.

Rebound decisions are often quick choices we make for the wrong reasons. Being clear on why we are doing what we are doing is the best guarantee not only of it being a good decision, but of it being beneficial in the long run.

Once you notice whether you subconsciously move toward or away from situations, you can determine if something is good for you or bad for you. In Phil's case, as he began to tap into his subconscious, he gained more clarity about why he wanted to move in the first place. Then, using both "The New You" hack (page 71) and the "Pivot" exercise (page 68), he was able to bring his subconscious and his conscious mind into better alignment and see the all-around benefit of his decisions. Yes—sometimes regrets are indications that our inner eight-year-old did not weigh in on a decision; other times, impulsive actions might stem from an overreactive subconscious not tempered enough by the conscious mind. The key to learning the principle of Moving Toward or Away is finding that sweet spot of balance between an active subconscious and a grounded conscious mind. The exercises in this chapter are designed to bring you into that balance.

When you tune into how you move toward or away, it becomes easier to notice any unhealthy patterns of behavior—codependent relationships, poor career choices, unhealthy friendships—that may be holding you back from realizing your dreams and achieving your goals. When Joanna, for example, recognized how turning away from more intimate connections with the men she dated had become a kind of habit, she made the first step to identifying her underlying fear of rejection. Indeed, she traced her habit back to a horrible, dramatic break-up when she was a mere sixteen years old—grief and disappointment from which she had not fully recovered.

When you learn how you move toward or away from people, places, and situations, your self-awareness grows, fueling your subconscious power.

In Principle Two, you tapped into your subconscious in order to begin to draw on its power. Now, in Principle Three, you are being asked to bring in your conscious mind to increase your awareness of your automatic patterns of behaviors and your entrenched attitudes that may be blocking your subconscious and/or undermining its natural alignment with your conscious mind. In order for us to feel centered, grounded, and nimble to make beneficial decisions and potentially big changes in our lives, we need the clean energy and compass of the subconscious, coupled with clarity of the conscious mind. By the end of this chapter, you will be one step closer to bringing your subconscious and your conscious mind into sync and clearing the path toward playing big.

Is This You?

As you attune to your thought and behavior patterns, ask yourself these questions.

Do you . . .

1. Find yourself in unhappy long-term relationships—work or personal?
2. Second-guess your choices?
3. Frequently bail on people?

4. Stay home when others go out?
5. Let your fear keep you from doing something?
6. Numb yourself with substances?
7. Have a negative attitude toward life?
8. Get stuck in thought-loops, in which you imagine negative outcomes to scenarios?

If you responded "yes" to any of these questions, then you may benefit from paying closer attention to how these behaviors or patterns may be holding you back. At one point in your life, these responses might have been useful or necessary to protect you. Now it's time to ask yourself, are they still working for you? Are they helping you or hindering you?

Understanding the Importance of Your Own Responses

Using the principle of Moving Toward or Away, you can gain further insight into your own dynamics. Margot is a good example. At thirty-five years old, she'd had a string of unsatisfying relationships—one after the other. One guy cheated on her, the next guy was verbally abusive, the next guy did both. You might say to yourself, *What's wrong with her? Why can't she see her destructive pattern?* That's the point. When we are in these patterns, it can be very difficult to stop the cycle. Why? Because we are unaware of how we participate in the creation of the patterns.

Am I "blaming" Margot for the abuse she suffered? Not at all! She was a having a *toward response*—but not to a situation/person that was ultimately good for her. When we worked together, one of the very first things we did was help her see from an objective distance what was subconsciously "attractive" about these guys, far under her radar. While in trance, I asked her, as I will encourage you to ask yourself, "What's working for you in these relationships/situations? What purpose does your dissatisfaction serve?"

For Margot, it was a matter of gaining insight into her own choices. Going after unattainable men meant she wouldn't have to face marriage. She harbored a deep-seated belief that marriage doesn't work. As different as the three different men were—one was a musician, the other worked as a chef, and the third managed a restaurant (and was married!)—they all enabled Margot to stick to her lack of trust in marriage or a solid, trusting relationship. In order to transform herself and her life, Margot would have to let go of this false belief and replace it with a more real and productive framing: that she deserved a solid relationship.

Here's another example. Two young sisters, ages fourteen and sixteen, from Arizona were approached by a music producer because he'd heard a demo of them singing. The younger girl, Audrey, was so excited because of a toward response: she longed for fame. The older sister, Tamara, had an away response: sure, she'd go to LA, but only to get away from the bullying girls in her tenth-grade class.

Audrey and Tamara's caretakers, their mother and grandmother, were motivated by their own toward/away responses. The mom had a toward response to moving to LA because she longed for financial independence for her daughters. The grandmother had an away response; she wanted to accompany her daughter and granddaughters to LA to get away from her history of poverty. Although all four people ended up happy (and successful!) in LA, they were clearly driven by different motivators. In other words, it's not always bad that we move away . . . it's only bad if it creates a problem.

Why is it important to understand their individual motivations? Because awareness breeds clarity, and clarity fosters good decision-making. It's a more direct path to *move toward* what you want, not blindly *away from* something you don't want.

Hypnotic Hack: Pivot

Change Your Patterns

Being aware of whether you are moving toward what's abundant and away from what drains you is a start. Try this exercise right now to practice a more intentional way to go toward your goals. This exercise fosters the clarity necessary for moving toward and away with intention.

1. Close your eyes and go within.
2. Imagine what you want to accomplish. See, hear, smell, taste, and feel it in detail. Ask yourself, are you primarily focused on moving toward this goal or away from something else?
3. Ask yourself what steps are necessary to achieve this goal.
4. Allow those necessary steps to reveal themselves.
5. Identify the resources you need.
6. What is the ideal timeframe to meet this goal?
7. Notice these steps orient toward your goal (as opposed to away from the past).
8. Are there any habits blocking you from this goal?
9. When a habit comes to mind, simply say inwardly "Thank

you for your service, you are no longer needed here."
(If a stubborn habit talks back—some do!—or seems
resistant to being released, let it be. It will eventually
release itself as you move forward through these pages.)

Revealing Our Patterns to Ourselves

Let's take a deeper look at how the patterns of our thoughts and behaviors play out in our lives.

One client immediately comes to mind. I'd known Greg for over twenty years. Handsome, successful, a big, warm personality. As a young man, he was a great athlete, playing basketball, tennis, squash— he could pick up any sport and become good at it quickly. Out of college he became a bond trader on Wall Street. He moved fast—both at work and after work. He partied hard, played hard, and worked hard. He married a lovely gal and they quickly had two children, a boy and a girl.

And then came the economic crash of 2008, and Greg's industry crumbled. At the time, he was approaching forty. His hard-living days were harder to recover from. And when his firm closed, it seemed like he had nothing positive or grounding in his life to balance out the pleasure-seeking. You can probably predict what happened to him: his earlier reliance on cocktails became abuse, and soon his pattern could be classified as outright addiction.

When Greg finally came to see me, he was feeling broken and out of control. I'd known him from afar as a good, happy guy. But the man who stood before me looked exhausted and frazzled, and was clearly in need of help. We first worked on his seeing the broad strokes of his behavior patterns: hard work (intense drive of conscious mind) needing emotional release (party hearty!), followed by downtime (recovery), only to repeat hard work, release, and recovery again and again. But at forty-two years old, his body and his brain were depleted and could not take that kind of abusive cycle anymore.

Addictive behaviors and attachment to negative habits are a repetitive numbing of the conscious mind and a subjugation of the subconscious. People who develop a dependence on a substance or activity—food, alcohol, drugs, shopping—typically use it originally as a coping mechanism that morphs into something that is no longer healthy. For Greg, it was alcohol; for Joanna, it was serial dating; others might develop a dependence on sweet, hyperpalatable foods. At first, these substances are not necessarily bad; it's when people turn to them to block feelings, or avoid issues, that the relationship to the substance becomes negative and sabotaging. Their need to numb themselves can be triggered by many different events or habits. Indeed, the causes in some ways don't really matter. What's significant is that people struggling against addictive tendencies are so out of balance and their conscious minds and subconscious minds so out of sync that they seek a negative, numbing state. Their need for numbing hijacks their body-mind systems, and they act in ways that hinder their ability to ultimately play big in their lives.

It was my mission to help Greg get more aligned with a healthy subconscious so that his conscious mind did not have to seek the drive, release, and recover pattern. I knew Greg could learn to integrate his subconscious to temper his drive to work hard so that his need for release was less intense. He was very often seeking trance, but using substances to get there.

Addictive behaviors are, in part, tied to a blocked subconscious—the conscious doesn't stand a chance of severing the cycle. And remember my own story of going General? I had become almost addicted to my need to be controlling; I had not only ignored the insight of my subconscious, but also was participating in a relationship that was hindering me: I was moving away from my true self and toward an inauthentic relationship.

I've used the following hypnotic hack to help people end cycles of negative, undermining habits. This can be used to stop smoking, drinking too much, nail biting, compulsive shopping, or any addictive habitual pattern.

Hypnotic Hack: The New You

This hack is all about where you are headed, as opposed to where you've been. Every day, new mornings dawn without our input, attitudes, opinions, oppositions. Just as the sun rises on a new day, so does the New You, ready to emerge.

You are ready. Simply reading this exercise is evidence that you are ready to quit a negative habit. Your subconscious and your conscious mind have decided this habit is not an indulgence; rather, it's a hindrance that has served its purpose and had its time. This is the time for a *NEW* and improved *YOU*. Tens, hundreds, thousands, and millions of people easily shed negative habits just like you will now.

As you prepare for a voyage, bring to mind your beautiful self, your perfect little eight-year-old self who is wise beyond his/her years. The desire you feel now to shed this behavior is your yearning to experience this wisdom. And keep in mind that you have the support system of the ages guiding you. Wisdom beyond the galaxies has brought you to this point of emergence, and you are deeply aware of this. On this important voyage, there are aspects of your behaviors you will need and those aspects or parts you will not need.

1. Close your eyes and go within.

2. Imagine before you a travel trunk, old and dilapidated . . . heavy, tired, and worn. In its prime it may have been useful. Now the hinges are rusty and disintegrating.

3. Bring to mind all the negative habits no longer needed for your voyage into greatness. One by one, lay each habit in the old, dusty trunk. (There is room in this trunk for any negativity you can imagine. No negative habit is too big to be put to rest here. You may speak to the habits or gesture to them; they are yours to dispose of now. Some may even speak back to you!)

4. Imagine that to the right of this trunk, a beautiful shimmering light is shining onto a large crystal platform.

5. Bring to mind all your positive attributes. One by one, approach each of these qualities as if they were magnificent crystal pillars to be erected on your crystal platform. Each pillar is strong and solid, shining brightly for the world to see.

6. Once you have erected your pillars of positive attributes, stand back and admire the glow.

7. Imagine this powerful glow forming into a beautiful crystal ball of swirling energy—a ball you will catch, with both hands, now!

8. Notice how the more your crystal ball ignites with possibility, the more the old, dark, and dusty trunk fades into the distance, until it completely disappears.

The glowing light has consumed everything around it, including you, until all negativity has completely vanished.

9. When it feels as if the crystal's energy has built to its maximum, imagine pulling that crystal orb into you. As you bring it within, you also bring in the universe's sources of wisdom, well-being, promise, hope, love, warmth, and security into your body, allowing all this positivity to light inside you. This crystal orb is you, your accomplishments, your dreams, your destiny. This lifetime is your voyage. You have all you need to propel you into greatness. Call on your pillars of strength often, reignite them regularly, run and play with this energy every chance you create. With this ignition, your new healthful habits will continue to evolve supporting your perfect soaring self!

Find Satiety

When your subconscious and your conscious mind are in sync, you don't need substances to fill you up, numb your feelings, or dull down the conscious. We all have a higher self and this part of us is accessible directly. You can access a more positive altered state on your own: meditate, attune yourself to nature, or practice yoga, remembering that these actions can also help you tap into trance. Each time you connect with your subconscious, you reinforce the likelihood that you will move toward what is good for you and away from what isn't beneficial.

As you try to leave non-helpful habits behind, you can also turn to your SoulSpirit for sustenance and support. Indeed, for many people, meditating, immersing oneself in nature, and practicing yoga are a communing with the SoulSpirit, which can also lead to true satiety. It will help you gain a more regular and tangible access to this higher plane of travel—a path with no tolls and no need of GPS. Try any one of these access points to the SoulSpirit:

- Walk in silence in a natural setting—the mountains, seaside, or a wide-open field.
- Submerge into water.
- Listen through headphones to your favorite song.
- Do a news or technology fast for several days.

Hypnotic Hack: Move Through Hesitation

We all can hesitate or procrastinate at times in our lives. Usually, the hesitation is a sign from your subconscious of some sort of emotional hitch—a question, doubt, or fear—about the pending activity. And obviously procrastination gets in the way of any movement at all—either toward or away. The key to getting past the hitch is to call upon your subconscious to reveal the source of the hesitation. This exercise can apply to big events in your life or the everyday chore that you always seem to put off. This hack utilizes your ability to ignite the responses you would like to have, whatever they are, and get you excited to move toward something desirable and fulfilling.

For example, say you have to move, and you are absolutely dreading having to pack. By using this hack, you can skip the state of being overwhelmed by all that you have to do to engineer the move.

1. Close your eyes and go within.

2. Imagine a scenario that you want to move toward but are currently hesitating to (e.g., a pending move).

3. Let your subconscious reveal the hitch: Is it packing the boxes? Choosing what goes and what doesn't? Is it the sadness of leaving a well-loved home behind? Whatever the feeling, acknowledge it.

4. Imagine the ideal scenario placed in front of you. Perfectly packed boxes, an easy move into your new home.

5. Brighten the colors, sharpen the sounds, and intensify the scents. Feel your happiness in your new home.

6. Intensify that image even brighter, bigger, and more defined.

7. Feel the heat and the momentum rising in your body as you imagine yourself in that place or situation.

8. Now release your brakes and zoom toward your goal.

This exercise can move you—mind, body, soul—through the emotional hesitation toward action. You can use this hack for situations big or small, important or inconsequential.

Use any sign that you may be procrastinating as a signal to pay attention: What is your subconscious trying to tell you? What might you need to move away from or toward?

Where Are You Now?

A significant step in empowering your subconscious is understanding your own toward/away responses to be sure you are attracting what you want and avoiding what you don't want. As you begin to uncover and listen to your subconscious, you will begin to tune into how you either approach situations or avoid them.

Sometimes you will discover that you are actually approaching situations that are *not* good for you and avoiding situations that are good for you. If you frequently procrastinate or think of yourself as very "laid back" or frequently experience "failure to launch," this may be you. In other words, when we are out of alignment, we can find ourselves in patterns that undermine our own happiness and essentially prevent us from our real desires.

Ideally, the more toward responses you create for yourself, the better your outcomes will be. Have you ever wondered why some racehorses wear side-blinders? Because their jockeys want them to focus on what's ahead of them—not what's on the side or to the rear. Distractions are risky.

Ask yourself, do you typically wake up looking forward to new challenges or circumstances, or do you wake up wanting to duck back under the covers? At times, we all need to move away from people and situations. This kind of move is beneficial and protective. I know plenty of new mothers who are completely attached to their infants but who yearn to get out of the house in order to be around other adults for social or intellectual stimulation. These new moms are moving toward socialization, not away from their babies. But how do you know when that posture is appropriate and when it is self-defeating? At every moment, we face a choice; if you want to steer your life instead of letting life steer you, you must also understand your orientation.

Now take some time to create an inventory of those behaviors or thought patterns that you'd like to discard and replace with more positive, life-affirming actions. Don't overthink this task; let your subconscious do the work for you. In fact, if it helps, close your eyes and go within, asking your subconscious to come forth. Then sit quietly with pen or pencil in hand (writing longhand is a much more direct route to the subconscious than using a computer or smartphone, but either will do). Make your list and then put it aside. We will return to it in the next chapter, when you build on this principle and learn how to cultivate more effective decision-making skills.

Where You Look, Your Focus Will Grow

As you learn to better understand your instinctual, automatic responses to the environment you live and work in, you will begin to develop more control over your conscious mind, giving you more leverage to direct your own destiny. Listen to the whisper of your subconscious and call for the SoulSpirit's guidance. Be present to your automatic behaviors that may no longer be useful to you.

And think about staying open and nimble. Imagine you are skiing downhill on an open powder trail. You have a wide white swath of snow in front of you. If you turn your head to the right, your skis will drift right. If you look toward the left, your skis will drift left. This may not even be conscious. The same goes for your subconscious: where you focus your energy is where you will grow your energy. This is a function of physics and also of how the subconscious and the conscious mind work in tandem to steer you in the best direction possible.

As you fine-tune your ability to move toward and away from what most benefits you, keep this image and metaphor in mind: you can train your conscious mind to look for the positive, the beneficial, the good. Your subconscious will not only follow, but also ensure that you're heading in the right direction.

As you prepare to explore the next principle, give yourself credit for the negative habits that you have moved away from and welcome the positive, life-enhancing decisions that await you.

Chapter 5

Principle Four:
Judge Thyself and Thy Neighbor

"You define yourself; don't let other people define you—that's a mistake."

—JUDGE JUDY SHEINDLIN

Like any one of her 11 million viewers, I'm a big fan of Judge Judy Sheindlin, known on television simply as Judge Judy. I have admired her for many years, and have even had the privilege of meeting her and have appeared on her show in the live studio audience. My admiration for her runs deep. On the surface, Judge Judy is a legal expert who uses her background in the family court system as well as her years of experience on the bench to enact judgment on the innocence or guilt of the people who stand before her in her TV courtroom. But everything she does as a judge is much richer and more nuanced than that: she brings together the weight of an exacting, rational conscious mind with a master's use of the subconscious to peer into human nature. Her capacity to both entertain us and satisfy our instinctual need for fairness, judgment, and resolution has made her viewership grow year after year.

The camera picks up on Judge Judy's clarity and presence. However, in person, she exudes softness, wisdom, and genuine beauty. A gorgeous glow emanates from her face, and she projects a serene sense of truth. If her robes were white, you might say she was angelic. Judge Judy is also an expert on the subconscious, using its power to pick up the information transmitted through the actions, expressions, attire, language, and, of course, evidence presented by her courtroom plaintiffs and defendants. Indeed, the soundness of her judgment stems as much from the sensory information gleaned by her subconscious as from the conscious mind and its ability to analyze the evidence and facts of a case.

What does this mean? Judge Judy is relying not only on the words people are saying or have written in their original sworn testimony, but on the nonverbal cues they are expressing. She listens and absorbs their tone, their pitch, and the nuances of cadence in their voices. She watches their facial expressions and hand gestures for clues as to who is withholding . . . and who is telling the truth. She takes in their appearance and watches their eye movements. She also observes their body language, including their posture, their positioning, and how they inhabit their bodies.

In one case I observed in person, a landlord sued a former tenant for nonpayment of rent and damages to the apartment. The landlord felt entitled to keep the tenant's deposit, and the former tenant was countersuing for return of that deposit. Judge Judy ruled for the landlord and, in addition, ordered the former tenant to pay the maximum small claims fine of five thousand dollars in damages. Why? Because in retaliation, the tenant had sent an obscene photo of a body part to the landlady's ten-year-old daughter. "You're a moron!" Judge Judy said, leaning forward dramatically. The tenant's poor judgment landed him with a maximum small claims fine. Judge Judy was teaching him a principle about the importance of learning how to use good judgment.

Obviously, the drama of her show highlights her skill at rooting out the good from the bad, the guilty from the innocent, the redeemable from those who may not be. However, what is relevant to our purposes here—using the subconscious to make life easier and more meaningful—is how to use the subconscious as a tool to ensure we make decisions that are in our best interest. We all make judgments, each and every second of the day, automatically appraising whether an event, situation, or person is good for us or bad for us. These types of judgment are automatic because they don't typically involve thought; they are emotional reactions that are hardwired into our brains. However, good judgment necessitates both clarity of conscious mind and the emotional truth of the subconscious.

Indeed, Judge Judy believes very strongly in this instinctual, emotional judgment. In one memorable case featuring a plaintiff's warring with the defendant over the rightful ownership of their dog, Judge Judy let the dog decide. Seeing how agitated the dog was in the defendant's arms, Judge Judy instructed the defendant to set the dog down. The dog immediately scurried to the plaintiff and Judge Judy announced to the woman, "That's it, she gets to take the dog home."

What goes unspoken but is abundantly clear is how Judge Judy prompts us, her audience, to ask ourselves some core questions: Are you aware enough of what you are doing? Are you aware enough of what others are doing? Do you know how to exercise good judgment for yourself?

The Importance of Good Judgment

In this chapter, we are going to see why this skill of judgment is so important for making decisions—big and small—and how judgment functions in our relationships with the people in our lives. From the point of view of the subconscious, judgment is a crucial player in determining what I call "goodness of fit" for any decision. Goodness of fit refers to how positive or healthy any decision's outcome will be for you. Determining goodness of fit or evaluating past decisions on this basis helps us to judge the impact of a decision so that we can learn from mistakes and repeat good decision-making. Learning to draw on both sources—the inner eight-year-old's sense of the emotional truth plus the Critical Thinker's more analytical perspective—to make our decisions is a crucial building block to playing big. In other words, judgment becomes essential to our well-being, our happiness and often our survival.

In this chapter, you will discover how we all have this capacity, but how, for many of us, it has become dulled by interference from too much stimulation in our social environment. We don't live in glass bubbles; we are in constant interaction with others, so we need to not only remain clear regarding our behaviors (how we move toward or away) but also how our emotions and internal biases affect our judgments and decisions. You're also going to learn how to strengthen this capacity for good judgment so that you can be more clear about the people in your life—are they a good fit? Are they trustworthy? Are they supportive?

Where Are You Now?

The previous three principles are intended to help you become more self-aware and tuned into your subconscious. In Principle One, you learn how to come into accountability, which requires that you be honest with who you are and where you are in your life right now. Principle Two primes you to connect with your subconscious and learn to trust your inner eight-year-old so that you can hear the whisper of this truth and prosper from the well of wisdom. In Principle Three, you begin to assess whether you move toward or away from people and situations; understanding your orientation helps you become aware of patterns that may be congruent with your subconscious . . . or working against it.

Now Principle Four will ask that you look both at yourself and outward, to your dynamics with other people—family, friends, colleagues, and mates and partners. Are you paying attention to what people are really saying? Do you need to reassess relationships or situations if they are not optimal for your personal ecosystem? Are you acting authentically for yourself? This principle enables you to maximize the power of the subconscious to hear the truth and actively pull your conscious mind into alignment so you can reliably make good decisions. This faculty of good judgment continues to activate the previous principles and moves you closer to being able to play big in your life.

Judgment Is Second Nature (and First in Command)

Scientists used to define judgment—aka decision-making—as a form of reward processing: if a decision was perceived as beneficial (i.e., rewarding), then we are motivated to decide and take action; if the outcome of a decision was perceived as negative (punishing or detrimental), it was assumed that we would not make that decision. And yet the reality of human behavior shows how this simplified model for understanding the *why* behind our decisions is much less black and white; indeed, many of us make many decisions that are clearly hurtful and/or harmful to ourselves and to others. The premise of this outdated view of decision-making is that we always act rationally.

Modern neuroscientists have begun to clarify the science behind decision-making, pointing out two major factors at play: 1) decisions and judgments are very much tied to emotions that lie under our conscious awareness and in our subconscious; and 2) most of us also possess biases that we are also unaware of and that affect how and why we make decisions. In the first case, the emotional roots of our judgments and decisions was demonstrated in a now famous 1997 card game study conducted by neuroscientist Antonio Damasio and others, which showed that participants who were deemed "good decision-makers" responded with sweaty fingers before they selected a card from a bad pile of cards. Their subconscious was picking up a signal that there was something wrong (a bad card at the top of the pile). The sweating is a "somatic marker" that is elicited before the conscious brain is aware of anything amiss. Indeed, the participants didn't consciously "know" it was a bad a decision until they turned over the card. This study and many following it get at the emotional nature of how we make decisions, pointing to their inherent subjective and almost irrational dimension, a line of research that Nobel Prize–winning thinker Daniel Kahneman has shown in his work and in his book *Thinking, Fast and Slow*.

Biases are those beliefs or attitudes that remain largely below conscious awareness but are so strong that they still shape our perceptions and impact how we predict the outcomes of decisions. In a now classic 1998 study by Greenwald, McGhee, and Schwartz of the University of Washington, fMRI scans of brain activity captured the existence of these "unconscious biases" that play out in our attitudes and beliefs toward people and situations. The outcome of this study was the creation of an actual test called the Implicit Association Test (IAT) that is still being used today to uncover latent prejudices, racism, or other stereotypical views of people.

What does all this mean? Our judgments are always subjective and vulnerable to our feelings, past experiences, and associations—much of which can remain buried in our subconscious. The point of this principle is to understand what is happening when we react inappropriately to a person or situation. Or when we don't leave a caustic or violent relationship. Or when we are attracted to situations that are sabotaging our happiness, draining our resources, or otherwise bad for us. Or when we freeze, unable to make a move or a decision. These are all obstacles that Principle Four will help you overcome.

In many of these cases, we are simply not paying attention to our subconscious.

A Different Kind of Judgment

In this era of mindfulness and tolerance, it's difficult to go against the grain and think about judgment as a positive thing. The word itself has become maligned, associated with treating people unfairly, profiling, or criticizing others because of an apparent difference. (Indeed, many of our opinions and attitudes reflect unconscious biases, as mentioned above.)

My use of the term "judgment" is different. I am using judgment in its most elemental, anthropological meaning, referring to the decisions we make. Judgment is not only good for us, it's also adaptive and purposeful, helping us make good choices for ourselves, which ultimately affects others in a positive way. Remember, we are all connected, so when our personal choices (stemming from our personal judgments) keep us ecologically sound, we thrive. Judgment is also about positioning yourself to play big: truly good decision-makers are those who play big.

The Goodness of Fear

What is happening when we don't use sound judgment? Gavin de Becker, author of *The Gift of Fear* and world-renowned expert on safety, stresses the importance of paying attention to any signal that elicits a fearful response—elevated heart rate, chills or goose bumps on the skin, flushed face. These physiological responses happen automatically because our brain-body system is responding to a certain situation or person that it recognizes as cause for concern. And our subconscious is a huge transmitter of this information. For this reason, fear cannot be ignored, and needs to be recognized as a friend and informant.

A few years ago, a young man approached me to help him prepare to surf the Banzai Pipeline on Oahu's North Shore; he wanted me to "make [him] unafraid." Without any hesitation, I told him no. Why not? Because it was irresponsible for me to help someone disregard his internal fear signals at his own potential peril. Fear protects us. Fear saves us. If this young athlete had gone into the pipeline, said to have claimed the most lives of any surf spot, without his fear signals intact, he would be putting himself in harm's way—and more than likely at death's door.

At the same time, some fears are reactionary or inappropriate and get in our way. Fear responses that don't have a purpose or are associated with a past experience that is no longer relevant can stress our brain-body systems. Think of the young child who wakes in the middle of the night, startled by the "ghosts" climbing on her bedroom walls. When she grows older, she realizes that what she saw were not ghosts but shadows cast by the streetlight below her bedroom window. If that little girl becomes a woman still afraid to sleep in the dark, she is carrying over an old fear, one that is no longer real, purposeful, or relevant.

Strong emotions such as fear, anger, and sadness are wired in defensive reactions designed to get our attention. When we don't heed their warning, we lose the message from the subconscious and information that is vital to our safety and well-being. Imagine for a minute that you did not have the capacity for sadness, and your mother, father, partner, or child is sick and in the hospital. Without sadness, you would overlook the need to protect this special person in your life. Anger signals that you detect some kind of unfairness. Fear signals that you may be in danger. These are important emotional messages that your subconscious emits to ensure your safety and well-being.

In his book, Gavin de Becker describes a woman who did not pay attention to the warning signals of a dangerous intruder because of the intentional ways the intruder masked himself and her unwitting denial of continual signals from her subconscious that all was not right.

Here's the scenario De Becker describes: a woman comes home to find the outside door of her apartment building ajar. Regardless, she enters, carrying several bags of groceries. As she begins to climb the stairs, one of the bags topples and a can of cat food rolls away. A man's voice calls from below, "Got it! I'll bring it up." She continues mounting the stairs to her fourth-floor apartment, listening as the stranger climbs after her. He offers to give her a hand, and she declines. He persists, asking what floor she was going to. Then he offers to help her collect the cans and help her out. He even tries to take one of the gro-cery bags. She repeats, "No, really, thanks, but no, I've got it."

Some part of her knows enough to deny his help, but another part of her is silent: the part of her that didn't want to be rude.

De Becker continues with his story, emphasizing that the woman was receiving signal after signal that all was not right with this stranger, yet she felt trapped by his insistence and physical presence. Eventually, he talks her into letting him inside her apartment to drop off the bags. He promises that he'll go. As De Becker writes, "She did let him in, but he did not keep his promise."

The story ends with the intruder tying up the woman at knifepoint and raping her.

So my question to you is why might this woman have ignored such red flags?

The woman in *The Gift of Fear* was so concerned with being per-ceived as polite, nice, and accommodating, she ignored the signal that danger was lurking up close and personal. This decision to remain polite instead of self-protective is a common reaction, especially for women. We can all find ourselves falling prey to the desire to look good in front of others or not be a bother or appear polite, and we inadver-tently put ourselves in harm's way or undermine ourselves as a result.

Obviously, the story of the woman on the stairwell is an extreme. But the lesson is a good one: take the time to pay attention to those signals so that you pull on both your subconscious and your conscious mind. Had the woman heeded the warnings that her subconscious was emitting, she might have hesitated to even go into the building, seeing that the usually locked door was ajar.

And one more point: I'm from the South, where we are taught to respect the words, "No thank you." Someone *not* respecting your "no" is *not* respecting you.

When we don't pay attention to or trust in our subconscious, we corrode our ability to pay attention to signals. The key here is to stay aware and heed the signals from the subconscious. I often suggest the hack "Upside/Downside" to assess the upside or downside of any interaction or encounter. In other words, is there more to gain or more to lose?

Hypnotic Hack: Upside/Downside

. . . .

1. Close your eyes and go within.
2. Imagine what you want. Do you want this person in your personal space? Is this person safe for you?
3. Now ask yourself what this person has to gain (he will want an exchange of some kind); identify the upside to the "give" or the downside to the "give."
4. Give your subconscious permission to weigh in and judge.

In the case of the woman on the stairs, she had more downside than upside to letting the man get close to her and help her. This hack can be useful in many situations to help call upon your subconscious; do it quickly in emergencies. It is helpful in aiding your everyday decisions—should you attend the party or not? Do you accept the invitation to have lunch with a new acquaintance or not? Upside/Downside has another function: it connects your subconscious to your conscious mind. The very act of asking yourself to consider the upside and the downside draws the subconscious and the conscious mind into alignment.

Hypnotic Hack: Let Go of Fears That Are in Your Way

. . . .

While fears can be clues that we are in danger, some fears actually get in our way. Keep in mind that fear is a feeling, and many fears are old reactions that no longer serve us. When a client comes to me because they are afraid of flying, I begin by asking about the trigger for the feeling. The plane gaining speed on the runway? Is it the takeoff? The sound of the wheels going up? Have they ever been in a plane crash?

Fears need to be unpacked so that you can get at the underlying threat response that happens automatically through your sympathetic nervous system. Neuroscientists and psychologists refer to the eradication of a threat response as "extinction." As you might predict, that's not a word I care to summon for anyone. However, the following Hypnotic Hack, which I adapted from hypnotherapy, acts on the same principle of desensitization. I've adapted it so that you preserve a positive communication with the subconscious and avoid introducing more fearful feelings.

Though quick and easy, this exercise creates powerful results. Depending upon your situation, you may want to repeat it until you no longer feel the fear reaction.

1. Sit comfortably, close your eyes, and go within.

2. Recall at what point you begin to feel fearful. (For example, if you're afraid of flying, isolate the moment that first triggers your fear response. Is it when you book your flight? Or walking down the Jetway? The sound of the engines during liftoff? If you're afraid of the ocean, is it putting on your swimsuit? If you fear

public speaking, is it when you are called onstage?)

3. Imagine you are sitting comfortably in your backyard or living room, watching a black-and-white film projected on an old barn door, the side of a house, or some rough surface. This film is out of focus, but you can see that you are the lead actor in this film. It's a comedy and everyone in the film is laughing hysterically at one another, including you! In fact, you can't stop laughing deep into your lungs.

4. You are watching yourself try to do the activity you were fearful of and as you watch yourself trying to do this thing, everyone continues to laugh at you and with you . . . everyone is so silly they are literally doubled over, laughing so hard.

5. Now run the same black-and-white film through your mind but *backward*. Everyone is walking backward, laughing backward, until you return to the beginning. You notice you are laughing so hard you can barely do this thing.

6. Try to access this old emotion of fear. Can you feel it? If so, run this model another time and recheck. When the model is run the correct number of times for you, you will have difficulty accessing the feeling of fear around the issue.

Fears are feelings attached to an automatic threat response deep in our limbic system. When you use your subconscious to interrupt the signal, the fearful feelings can be lessened or removed altogether.

The Power of Emotions

We are always impacted by those around us and must learn to navigate them, understanding their purpose in our lives, the dynamics involved, and to what degree these dynamics affect us. I always remind clients that if their mate is unhappy, there's little chance they will be happy. If a child is unhappy, the parent's own happiness will be limited. And so on. When we are not tuned into or acting from our subconscious, we can take on the tenor or mood of the other person, which in turn interferes with our good judgment.

Look around you: how many relationships do you know that are caught in an unhealthy dynamic because one person is undermining the other, or is too controlling, or is too submissive, or is antagonistic and sarcastic? Think of the uptight coworker who affects the mood of the entire office. The hypersensitive sister who drags everyone at the family gathering into her well of despair. If we are not careful, we can take on these negative moods of others. We can also let our own negative feelings overshadow us and complicate our ability to make healthy, life-affirming decisions.

Barry was a military man, having served two tours in Iraq and returned home to the United States a more mature person. Unlike many of his fellow soldiers, Barry was lucky—he had escaped the ravages of PTSD; however, he did reach out to me because of problems he was having getting along with others at work. He was a midlevel manager at a posh, successful restaurant chain.

"I think I have a problem," he burst out.

When I asked him to elaborate, Barry explained, "I think everyone is the enemy." He had tears in his eyes, and I could see he was in turmoil.

I knew one of the first things Barry needed to do was tap into his subconscious and commune with that inner eight-year-old who was buried under all his military training. He needed to soften and let his subconscious speak more directly to him.

Once he was hypnotized and relaxed, I asked him to use his judgment to evaluate the people with whom he worked. I could see they weren't the problem, but it was important for Barry to understand this perception for himself.

Going through the exercises (see the "Practice Good Judgment" and "Positive/Negative Charge" hacks on pages 95 and 105), Barry was able to acknowledge the pain, loss, and fear he had experienced throughout his time in the military. Through our work together, he was able to cry, mourn, for that "young kid who signed up." Still proud of all his accomplishments, he was also able to move past the hurt and stop judging himself so harshly. Together, we released this "soldier Barry" from duty. And by reconnecting with his inner eight-year-old, Barry was able to diffuse his harsh judgment of himself, which in turn disabled his habit of judging others harshly. He began to get along much better with others, especially at work.

Granted, it's much easier to see how others make errors in judgment and repeat such mistakes again and again. Looking at our own errors is infinitely more challenging. However, it can be done; when you take the time to acknowledge how you are feeling about a decision, relying on your subconscious to make your feelings clear, then you are more likely to use both parts of your mind equally and thereby make good choices and practice good judgment.

Pay attention to how the subconscious and the conscious mind treat judgment differently:

- The subconscious practices swift justice. Think of playground politics: if Johnny hits Sal, Sal is going to take a swipe at Johnny. Deciding and judging happen simultaneously.

- The conscious mind is more rational and mature, taking a more measured approach to deciding and judging.
- The conscious mind is more comfortable with ambiguity and gray areas, able to wait and see what unfolds.
- The subconscious wants resolution and can be selfish, operating solely from its own point of view.

It's using both the conscious and subconscious that protects us and our well-being. For instance, if you're having a difference of opinion with a coworker, you don't lunge at him in the elevator and bite him. You think through the situation carefully, from the perspective of office politics, your immediate goal of doing your job, and how you can still maintain the upper hand in terms of leverage. But in listening to your subconscious, you act and do something—you don't sit around and wait. An overactive subconscious might respond impulsively, in a too-heightened state of emotion. Good judgment happens when you use all of your mind's capacities.

For example, a person who is sick with a debilitating illness may be hampered by depression and a sense of helplessness. These feelings heighten her sensitivity and may influence her to make rash decisions. Mary was in just this position. Diagnosed with breast cancer, she felt overwhelmed, angry, and depressed all at once. Underneath all those feelings was fear. "I'm not ready to die! This is not fair!" she said to me. Through our work with Hypnotic Hacks, she was able to get in touch with these feelings and begin to process all her emotions. Once she was calmer, she was able to come to a decision that made her feel secure: she chose to switch doctors and allow her daughter to come live with her for a few months. And it all worked out: her cancer was not terminal. Mary did not even require surgery, and made a full recovery after several months of treatment.

Oftentimes it takes a lot of practice before we can trust our own judgment. We might make some mistakes by listening to others instead of ourselves or simply disregard our own gut feelings. And yet the more you subconsciously tune into what's before you—in a person or a situation—the more you can practice *full* judgment, drawing upon both your conscious mind and subconscious emotional truth. This goes back to giving you less to do—less complications, less rerouting, a less complicated life, less heartache, less detriment to others. This awareness will guide you on your path.

Hypnotic Hack: Practice Good Judgment

The more you trust your subconscious and listen to its insight and wisdom, the deeper your capacity for good judgment.

This exercise will help you go through the motions of good judgment; practice makes perfect! If I could wave a magic wand to remove all the ill will, heartache, and bad vibes that ensue from not using good judgment, I would. Instead, try this quick exercise. *This* is your wand. This exercise can be applied to one issue or a group of issues. As you close your eyes and go within, let your subconscious bring to mind that which needs your attention.

1. Close your eyes and go within.
2. Imagine any part of your life that feels tight or disturbing—anything that is not working. Call it to mind.

3. Ask yourself, *How did I cause this situation?* (You may want to refer back to Principle One, "Come into Accountability.")

4. Allow all your steps of poor judgment to rush forward. They will.

5. This new awareness gives you permission to correct the misjudgment.

6. Allow a replay of the corrected decision to happen (this occurs at mind speed).

7. Ask yourself, *Would I know better now? What would need to happen to not repeat this behavior in the future? Would I make better judgments in the future?*

8. If the answer is "no," repeat this exercise until you feel confident that you'd act with better judgment in the future.

This hack will help you understand errors in judgment, which is another way to think about our mistakes. Just as you did in Principle One, "Come into Accountability," it's up to you to own your errors in judgment, so you can clear your path and stay close to your subconscious power. The occasional lapse in judgment (i.e., mistake) happens; we're only human, after all. But the real issue is making the same error in judgment over and over again. Repeated bad judgments not only drain your energy but also block your capacity to enjoy your life. When you use this exercise to pinpoint your lapses in judgment, certain threads and patterns of behavior will become evident, just as they did when you were recognizing how you move toward or away.

The Power of Nonverbal Cues

So how do we practice judgment using our subconscious? The more socially complex and evolved our world becomes, the more important it becomes to be able to decipher situations and people. The world we inhabit today is very unlike the world occupied by previous generations, where people were much less mobile and you generally knew someone through their family or other community connections. Now many people move away from where they were born. This distance from our families and original communities seems to correspond with people becoming more skilled at masking, hiding, or misrepresenting their intentions. Judgment is an essential skill, because we need to exercise judgment about people in various situations, in different ways. For instance:

- A person may approach you in a crowded store, asking for help—are their intentions transparent?

- You're interviewing a young woman or man for a babysitting or housekeeping position—are they trustworthy, hardworking?

- You're at a social event and you're introduced to a man/woman as a prospective date—would this person be a good match, or is he/she a good person?

- You're making your selection of who will be part of a committee—will the new candidate be a good fit for the group, and a helpful contributor?

To make the best judgment in each of these scenarios, you need to rely on more than a résumé or what people are actually saying out loud. To make the best possible decision, you need to read people and cue into what they are not saying out loud and may only be suggesting. In other words, you need to recognize the subconscious signs they are giving you, and tap into your own subconscious to ascertain a complete picture of who this person is and what his or her intentions are. So how do we tune into our subconscious and train our conscious awareness to make better judgments?

Just like Judge Judy, you will rely on the nonverbal communication skills that give you information about people. These so-called soft skills (empathy, ease with people, mind reading, to name a few) and the nonverbal communication cues that hint at people's thoughts, feelings, and biases are enormously important to functioning in our daily lives. Going back as far as Charles Darwin and B. F. Skinner, and continuing into modern-day neuroscience, anthropology, and behavioral economics, researchers have underscored the importance of these instinctual ways we infer information and assess people. You might refer to these skills as your "people skills" or your "gut feelings" about someone. These are not random or arbitrary signals; these are very real channels through which we gather clues about other people—their feelings, their motives, their frame of mind.

Researchers have shown that an increased awareness of nonverbal skills helps reveal someone's agenda. So far, psychologists and cognitive scientists have identified nine different nonverbal modes of expression: eye contact, facial expressions, tone of voice, body language, gestures, use of space, touch, and artifacts. Some of these modes of communication may seem familiar; yet using your subconscious awareness brings another level of nuance to these methods of understanding people, and will ultimately enable you to hone your judgment to discern their goodness of fit for you and your life.

Let's take a look at how to listen to your subconscious to read people more accurately:

1. **Eye contact/gazing:** Docs a person look you straight in the eye? Is he or she able to maintain eye contact? Does he or she avert his gaze? Blink excessively? Eyes have always been considered the windows of the soul, and for good reason. Some scientists suggest that hard staring is an indication of lying; others will say averting is a lie—either could be true . . . or not. Gaze is often a reflection of a cultural norm; regardless of its context, it's important to call upon your instincts to discern how best to interpret these cues.

2. **Facial expressions:** Is a person smiling? Frowning? Can you detect a mood from someone's face? In general, scientists have agreed upon the existence of five basic emotions: happy, sad, angry (disgusted), afraid, and ashamed. Of course, within these categories there are thousands of micro-feelings. The psychologist Paul Ekman, who was a pioneer researcher in facial expressions and emotions, has identified over three thousand micro-expressions representing discreet emotional states. Why is this significant? Because, as Ekman suggests, people often are not saying what they really mean. They will mask or hide or outright lie about their true feelings. Why is this important to keep in mind? It behooves us to pay attention to more than just one nonverbal cue to glean someone's intention or orientation.

3. **Tone of voice:** What's in a tone of voice? Personality! Emotion! Tone gets at the emotion behind someone's words and includes degree of loudness, pitch, and inflection. When we encounter people or situations and need to size them up, it's crucial to pay attention to tone of voice. This may seem commonplace, but there's so much more under the surface. Does someone end a sentence in an "up tone" or with a question? This pop culture dialect points to a new way of connecting. Ending a sentence on a question invites openness. Similarly, mimicking tone and pace is an efficient way to extend rapport.

4. **Body language and posture:** Social scientists have been studying body language for decades. In her book *Presence*, social scientist and TEDx speaker Amy Cuddy suggests that "power posing" not only connotes strength and confidence but can also impact relationship dynamics, in business and otherwise. Hypnotists and psychologists have known the "big reveal" of body language for years, and how we live in our bodies reflects so much about who we are . . . and how we feel about ourselves. When you begin to look outward, assessing and judging others, consider their body language—and the sense of self it may reveal underneath. You can determine how receptive or open a person is to you. Are his arms crossed or uncrossed? Is her torso leaning toward you or away? You can also examine photos for clues as to how comfortable someone is with others in the photo. How are people oriented in the photo? Close, keeping their distance? Is a smile coming from the eyes or just the mouth? An authentic smile has nothing to do with your mouth and

all to do with how it lights up your eyes. The subconscious is very attuned to symbolism—and body language is a powerful symbol.

5. **Gestures:** The way we use our hands when we speak reveals personality and style. Think of the excitement conveyed by a soul-filled TV evangelist, the calmness embodied by the two clasped hands of the Dalai Lama, or the aggressive rejection when someone puts a hand up to indicate "stop!" Our gestures are impactful ways we communicate meaning and intent, and learning to attune to the gestures of others will provide you with helpful information related to that person's state of mind. For example, gestures can signal "I'm willing to help," "Stay away, you're bothering me," or "Please come here."

6. **Use of space:** This mode of nonverbal communication is quite interesting. Think about how you position yourself in meetings, on a date, at a big party. Do you like to be up close and personal? Do you prefer to keep yourself at least at arm's length? If you're on an elevator, are you bothered when someone brushes up against you? Now flip these questions around: What might it say about someone if she "invades" your personal space during a first or second meeting? Is there too much familiarity? Assumed intimacy? What might this use of space suggest? Do you know there's one power seat at every table? This is the old-style "head of the table"—the head is where the focus naturally goes. The person who sits at the actual head of the table (the very ends of a rectangular table) takes the most powerful seat in the room. It's a posture that connotes power, a demand for respect, and a desire to control.

7. **Touch:** Have you ever been seated at a table—in an office or at a restaurant—and noticed someone twirling her hair? Or cracking his knuckles? Or playing incessantly with his phone, pencil, or digital device? People who touch their own bodies and/or inanimate objects are showing signs of self-soothing. Science shows that this kind of activity is a way to distract a person from his or her own nervousness, agitation, or discomfort—physical or emotional. On the other hand, when people touch other people, they are showing a desire to connect or be listened to. It's a form of intimacy—the back slap by one of the guys, taking a child's hand when walking on the sidewalk, a romantic clasp of the hands during a movie. Touch connotes intention one way or another.

8. **Appearance:** Your clothes tell a story, as do your hair, fashion, your general kempt-ness, and other ways you present yourself. We all vary in our personal style and fashion sense—thank goodness for diversity! When you're getting to know someone or evaluating them at this automatic level, how someone appears to you and the details you take in and analyze coalesce to give you a singular impression. This is what love at first sight hearkens back to. This is what a strong negative reaction to a first-time meeting can be about. Appearance matters on so many levels . . . more than we think consciously. When you dress in the morning, you are creating your outward statement about how you either want to feel or be perceived by others. Fashion is based on this premise, and women and men spend millions of dollars and many hours choosing clothes to communicate their self-image, their desire to fit in or stand out, and their value or self-worth.

9. **Artifacts:** Tattoos, jewelry, avatars, and logos—these are all symbols people use to signify some aspect of themselves. What do these visual signposts of personality, tribes of connection, or representations mean? Are they truthful reflections of who we are or who we aspire to be? Our objects and symbols hold great value.

Assessing the People in Your Life

Judge Judy relies on these nonverbal cues to literally judge people. Using her instincts and insight into what nonverbal cues reveal about the people in her courtroom, she reflects back to the audience what she is seeing, providing a kind of mirror onto the accused. In one thirty-minute program, the ordinary person's daily life is magnified and the audience is treated to a kind of laboratory experiment where they get to witness how other people make mistakes and either use their judgment or not.

You can apply the setup or architecture of Judge Judy's show to your everyday ordinary experiences by simply looking at others not as if they are guilty of some kind of crime or misdemeanor, but as revealing clues about their goodness of fit for you.

I recommend that you think of the people in your life like paintings or pieces of art that make up a collection. With every new person we bring into our lives, our subconscious considers where in our "house" any one piece of art might fit and how it makes us feel. What slot does this person fill or fit into? If you look at your dwelling as your nest or cave, any smart animal would not invite in random individuals, right? The same applies to those people you allow into your life.

You also want to consider how close you bring people in. Those friends you'd invite to a backyard barbecue are probably not the same that you'd invite to a holiday dinner. Think of all the people who make up the art collection of your life. (In chapter 10, you will focus on the people in your life as the Energetic Circle of Influence and learn to more categorize individuals so that you can determine their place in your life—whether they are intimately close [inner], socially close [middle], or more on the perimeter of your life [outer].)

For now, consider the people present in your life today, those who have informed your life in the past, and those you may invite in in the future, think about how and why you bring some in closer than others. Some of us need to be more wary than others. I've observed that many single women, when they are hungry for companionship, might let their guard down and invite in people who are not a good fit, or who may even be dangerous. Some of my male clients who use online dating services become vulnerable to "catfishing," prowling singles who misrepresent themselves and their intentions. We all have our blind spots.

So as you consider the array of people who populate the colorful collection of your life, think of your choices in terms of their congruence. Are certain people more or less congruent with the other art on your walls? Do certain people stand out in a good, special way? Or do they stand out in a negative way? Does the overall array of art round out what you have collected, or are some colors too loud and overwhelming for your palette? The people in our lives reflect our judgments and assessments of who is important, who is trustworthy, and who is supportive.

Don't be an open door to everyone. With our lives being lived so openly on social media, our devices recording our voices, and our phones using facial recognition, it becomes more important than ever to protect our privacy, regardless of how the "internet of things" might mesmerize us. Our privacy is important, and we have the right to protect it. You should be discerning. Indeed, it concerns me that we've dulled our primal edge and lost our sense of predators and privacy. Judging goodness of fit applies not only to people in our lives but to activities as well. Psychologists have been noticing a generational difficulty in establishing healthy boundaries because of how much time we spend living life online, in full public view. Numerous studies have linked depression and anxiety with exposure to social media. The line between how many likes we might get and real friendships has become blurred. The CDC reports female teen suicides have hit a forty-year high, and this statistic is directly related to social media maladjustments, including anxiety and depression. Male adolescent suicide is on the way up as well. A steady stream of dopamine hits to the brain in the form of visuals and new posts literally has us addicted. If this is you, I do believe time away from tech can be restorative.

But we are all vulnerable to the responsibility presented by communicating through technology. Meetings in person have become less and less frequent. Instead of applying for jobs in person, many people simply upload a résumé through a giant list server; actors now send in videos of their scenes rather than showing up in person to audition. This loss of face-to-face, in-person interaction interferes with our use of animal instincts for reading another person's nonverbal cues; people can't use their animal magnetism to mesmerize a romantic interest as easily; and ultimately, people might not be able to connect in fully personal ways.

Hypnotic Hack: Positive/Negative Charge

This quick, simple, and highly effective exercise should be used to assess someone new to determine if a prospective friendship or relationship is a good fit for you. When done correctly, the person you are judging will not be consciously aware of your assessment. Next time you meet someone new, try the following:

1. Shake hands, greet, or say hello, offering connection and sending energy toward the other person. Next, consciously pull all your energy back into your body.

2. How does this person *feel* to you now?

3. Do you notice a warm = positive feeling? Do you notice a cold or chilly = negative feeling?

Your subconscious will tell you if a person is safe or good for you based upon the degree of warmth or coldness. A cold feeling means the person is probably not a good fit for you right now; hence a negative charge. A warm feeling means he or she gives off a positive charge for you right now.

The Positive/Negative Charge hack can be used frequently and should be. People change, situations change, and so do you. The warm/cold feeling or positive/negative charge may be different depending on the circumstances or even your frame of mind. It is not necessarily a fixed judgment on the other person.

Again, in chapter 10, you will dive deeper into all your relationships; for now, consider this hack as a way to fine-tune your skill of judgment, which is for you and you alone. Your subconscious will take in and download all the information at record speed so you will have a quick cheat-sheet on the positive/negative encounter with this person and whether this person is ecological and healthy for you now or perhaps later. Whatever it is you find in him or her—pleasing or displeasing—on the deepest level, you will know.

Awareness = Freedom

When you think you're operating alone, remind yourself you are not—we are always affected by those around us. The key to staying closely in sync with your subconscious is to decide who is helpful and who is a hindrance. Use your judgment to surround yourself with people who bring out the best in you.

Exercising good judgment also means reacting appropriately to situations. In other words, plug into your subconscious to feel the truth of your emotions, then call upon your conscious mind and its ability to discern right from wrong. I'm reminded of one of many wise adages from Oprah Winfrey. This one in particular has always resonated with me: "Doubt means don't. Don't move. Don't answer. Don't rush forward." This is the subconscious sending you a message, refining your sense of judgment.

On this journey of self-awareness, becoming more tuned into the people around you enables you to make better, more constructive choices. When you know who someone is, you are more likely to honestly assess their goodness of fit. In many ways, this essential act of judgment is what keeps you out of trouble and enables you to sidestep problems or negative situations that could have been easily avoided.

Life does not have to be a minefield, and you don't have to be a ballet dancer, fearfully tiptoeing across a slippery stage. You simply need to listen to the voice of truth within you.

Chapter 6

Principle Five: Give to Get

"If one gives food to others, one will improve one's own lot . . .
if one lights a fire for others, one will brighten one's own way."
—BUDDHA NICHIREN DAISHONIN

Getting what you want out of life necessitates accepting that you are entitled to get it. Yes, *get!*

You may not yet be comfortable with this new concept of giving to get. I understand; we live in a culture that venerates selfless giving. But is giving without expecting something in return actually good for anyone? This chapter is all about enacting one of the most important principles that ensures you can and will play big in your life. You will learn how give to get is not selfish, but self-full. You will discover not only the power to give purely but also how expecting something in return is good for all of us, pulls us together, and unites our sense of connection throughout the universe.

Indeed, it's time to drop the martyr act, forgo the impulse to give without the expectation of something in return, and grant yourself permission to go after all of what you imagine to be yours. Yes—all that you desire can be achieved *if* you embrace this principle based on reciprocity.

Doesn't it make sense that your success and happiness depend on how well you can identify what you truly want and need, and then go and get it? Your dreams won't just be delivered to you on a silver platter. The person who has no energy, willpower, or drive to go after what he or she wants won't get very far. And you will notice that oftentimes these un-achievers are also not true givers. Why? Because givers are *doers*, not talkers and takers.

In this chapter, I'm going to explain what makes some people able to dream big, go after what they want, and then actually enjoy the results of their labor. As I've seen again and again in my practice, my most successful clients exhibit three essential traits that are all inexorably linked to this principle of give to get and its reciprocity:

- A belief that they can do anything they set their minds to with the cooperation of others; cooperation is what enables any type of community—from tribe to city to nation—to thrive; cooperation underlies civility and is the backbone of our connection to one another.

- A strong acumen for whom they can trust; in order to give to get, you must use your subconscious power to judge those in your orbit.

- An inherent sense of fair play; when we give to get, we reinforce the universal mandate of treating others with the highest integrity and honoring the essential fairness of reciprocity.

These are the three key tenets that are essential to learning how to use the principle of give to get. Though our subconscious instinctively acts from a place of cooperation, trust, and fair play, the conscious mind learns how to use reciprocity over time and sometimes through a bit of trial and error. And yet its importance cannot be underesti-mated: Reciprocity is what enables us to truly ask for what we want from life; it helps us to see our opportunities and leverage situations and relationships to our best advantage, without taking advantage of someone else. This ability to ask, to give, and to get is the ultimate en-actment of playing big. It's a win-win for all and propagates fairness. The subconscious knows this; our conscious mind needs explicit in-structions and practice.

The Science Behind Beneficial Exchange

Did you know that even primates share a sense of fairness? In an in-teresting experiment, two researchers, Sarah Brosnan and Frans de Waal, published an article in *Nature* (2003) called "Monkeys Reject Unequal Pay." In the study, they created a number of pairs of capuchin monkeys and trained them to expect a food reward in exchange for a rock. Once in pairs, each monkey was given a rock; if the monkey gave back the rock when prompted by the scientist, they would receive either a grape or a piece of cucumber. The scientists quickly observed that the more valued reward was the grape. When both monkeys in the pair were given the same reward—whether grape or cucumber—they would both continue to participate in the rock-for-food exchange game. However, if one monkey in a pair was given a favored grape and the other was given a cucumber, the monkey who received the less-desirable cucumber would refuse to cooperate further.

The scientists use this series of experiments to support the notion that "cooperation is propelled by two biological engines: kin selection and reciprocity."

What does this mean for our give-to-get principle? We all are

aware of fairness and will have a reaction to situations we deem un-
fair. In fact, we all have a negative reaction to an overt lack of cooperation. We *all* benefit when people behave in a cooperative way and
have an automatic negative reaction to an overt lack of cooperation.
In other words, we work best when we can trust that all in a group
behave cooperatively. We rely on this give and take in many types of
transactions in our everyday lives. Employer and employee; landlord and renter. I "friend" you, you "friend" me back. I "follow" you,
you "follow" me. These are all mutually beneficial arrangements that
are meant to work for both parties and in this way complete an energetic circuit. The give-to-get principle is what motivates people in
church to join hands, or inspires communities to come together and
work toward a common goal. It's what ties neighbors together—the
sheer proximity assumes cooperation and reciprocity. Give to get
builds communion and invites all parties to take part. Essentially,
this study and others like it show how all social groups rely on cooperation to operate in a trusting, orderly way—whether that social
group is two people in a relationship, a nuclear family of three or
four, a team, an office of colleagues, or a nation. Indeed, the closer
the circle, the more likely it is that we extend trust and need that
trust.

Scientists even have a name for our disdain for lack of cooperative
fair play; they call it "inequity aversion." Think of how we denigrate
cheating on the sports field. Or lying in the courtroom. We are quick
to judge (think of Principle Four!). Brosnan and de Waal and other
social scientists also emphasize that cooperation and mutual altruism
is expected in humans and other species.

In other words, we expect some kind of exchange for both our
willingness to cooperate with the group and our participation. Indeed,
Brosnan and de Waal explain that many of our "basic emotional reac-

tions and calculations" that define our sense of fairness seem tied to our evolutionary roots.

Anthropologists have known for years that many species, especially those that are most closely related to humans, like primates, exhibit such "prosocial" cooperation. They have observed again and again how animal packs or families voluntarily share their food, care for one another's young, and groom one another. Our early ancestors (hunters and gatherers) may not have lived in our complex social systems, but they showed this "prosocial" cooperation in an even more advanced way, including voluntary food sharing; caring for infants, the elderly, and the sick; and an equitable division of labor and sharing of responsibilities. All these customs were taught by elders to the young so the group or tribe as a whole got along, stayed safe, and experienced a day-to-day sense of well-being. This cooperation and implicit trust also positioned a tribe for better prosperity. What greater vulnerability might there be to a tribe than in-fighting? Any enemy could take advantage of discord by potentially splitting off some members. Again, these behaviors underscore not only how innately social we are, but also how interdependent we are.

We see this same cycle in nature as well. Think of the fruit tree. The healthier the soil, the more fruit it will bear. Even the dying tomato on the vine feeds the soil and gives nutrients back to the earth for future fruit; even in death there is a give, a purpose. The two need each other to exist and prosper. The cooperative nurturing happens at all levels of our ecosystem. And of course, we know that the more well cared for our young are, the more likely they will survive long enough to reproduce. Our caring for one another is not simply altruistic; it's fed by an ulterior purpose, which, at the most elemental level, is successful survival. The problems ensue when one party breaks the circuit.

Where Are You Now?

Principle Five drove home the importance of developing good judgment and making decisions that are in your best interest and keep you safe. It also strengthened your ability to judge how supportive and healthy your relationships are for you, and better decide whom to let into your life and whom to cut out of it.

Our relationships play various roles in our lives, so we don't have the same expectations for all of them. However, all healthy, balanced, equitable relationships—whether intimate or distant, social or professional, friendly or familial—rely on trust, spirit of cooperation, and fairness. And they all, at some level, will eventually drill down to the give-to-get principle.

So think about your own relationships. Do they feel reciprocal? Are you doing too much giving? Too much asking for favors without giving back? As you read on, begin to filter through your relationships with family, friends, colleagues, and acquaintances. And as you do, begin to determine what you really want to ask for from others and the universe at large.

The Trap of Overgiving

I have a confession: I am a recovering overgiver. I spent many years and tremendous amounts of energy dreaming up gifts for family, friends, colleagues—not to mention men I loved and dated. I was very invested in coming up with the perfect gift to show just how well I knew the person on the receiving end. And boy, was I good at this! I was the person who dreamed up perfect gifts for my girlfriends and family members; the person who went out of her way for others, even when it was a massive inconvenience to my own life; the person who believed that giving meant more than receiving.

Most of you probably have felt this way at one time or another in your life. I looked at my own giving from all angles to rationalize and justify it, but it all boiled down to one false belief: *If I give more, then I will be loved more.* I couldn't have been more wrong. I was the one creating imbalance by giving too much—I was giving desperately in order to get support and love. I treated gifts like a royal event, giving loved ones everything under the sun. If it floated, flew, or drove—I gave it. I had set up an unhealthy dynamic in which every occasion had to be more special than the next, every gift more superlative than the last. I wanted to outdo myself. If I had respected my own instincts, my own boundaries, I would have known that people, in general, are in no way capable of keeping up with me, nor should they. Sometimes, recalibrating your urge to give asks that you discern between the people who are not truly reciprocating and those who are. This does not mean we can all give in the same way or to the same degree; this is really about the thought or intention behind any gift mattering most.

In my desperation, I was giving without receiving and unwittingly creating a negative cycle. The night I heard John on the phone, I started the process of ending that cycle.

It took me years before I finally saw my overgiving nature as something that was actually hurting me. Of course, some of my relationships were not only fair and reciprocal, but very loving and meaningful. However, many were not—with a common denominator. I realized that I was extending too much of myself without expecting enough in return.

Mothers are classic overgivers. Women who take on traditional roles as nurturers and family caregivers often fall into behaviors where they give up too much of their time and energy for the betterment of the family. The result? Women often find themselves depleted and often bitter. Think of Shel Silverstein's classic children's story *The Giving Tree*, in which the little boy keeps asking his favorite tree to give him part of itself—shade, apples, and later, when the man is an adult, the tree's limbs and finally its trunk. By the end of the story, the tree is a lonely stump with nothing left to give. The irony? The man is even more bereft and bitter—old and alone, sitting by himself on the stump of the tree from which he has taken so much.

Although it's common to fall into the game of martyrdom, it's actually unnatural at a subconscious level. The subconscious understands that overgiving puts the self in peril; instead of being an act of generosity, the act of giving becomes an act of depletion of the self.

The Transactional Nature of Give to Get

Any healthy relationship must be founded on trust, fairness, and equanimity—the basis of reciprocity and the give-to-get principle. One client comes to mind. Lori was in a longtime marriage to Mac and told me about an incident that occurred around her fiftieth birthday. She and Mac were in line to pick up her prescription at the drive-through window of a pharmacy. Mac pulled up to the window and the pharmacist asked for Lori's date of birth. Mac hesitated and gave a date—October 23, 1965. As his face flushed and it was clear that he was embarrassed, Lori realized that after all those years of marriage, he didn't remember her birthdate. She felt a crush of hurt and humiliation—for herself and for Mac.

As Lori described the event to me, she said she noticed a succession of thoughts: for the past several years, Mac had not given her a single gift, not even a card. Of course he wouldn't remember her birthdate. But then Lori realized that it was actually her fault he didn't remember her birthday. She went back to Principle One, accountability: she had allowed him to get away with not acknowledging her birthdays whatsoever. She had allowed him to not celebrate her birthday. Lori had never held Mac accountable; she had zero expectations from him, even for a birthday card. She had let give to get slide in many ways.

In retrospect, Lori knew she needed to let him know how important it was to her that he remember and celebrate her birthday, instead of letting birthdays come and go without expressing how she felt. Not talking to him about her feelings was a form of dishonesty.

This is a perfect example of how giving (of yourself) without expecting anything in return undermines a relationship. The energy cannot flow in a broken circuit. Lori was energetically giving Mac a free pass in the relationship—taking away his opportunity to complete the loop. She was giving of herself on his birthdays without expecting a return from him—his time, energy, and attention—on her birthdays.

Your birthday may not be important to you or your mate, but other occasions are important to you. Maybe it's having someone take care of you when you're sick. Or coming home to a warm meal after a long day of work. Or having someone bring you coffee in bed every morning. This story isn't about birthdays, but about the principle of giving—and how important it is to give *and* receive.

Counter to what we're often raised to believe, giving selflessly only hurts you and the authenticity of your relationships. Would the Uber driver drive you around town without charging you? Would you show up to your job day after day, week after week, month after month with no paycheck? If a relationship is one-sided and not reciprocal, it begins to devolve, grow old, stale, or even destructive. It's a matter of perspective and a judgment call.

When I stopped being the giver extraordinaire, when I took my own advice and truly embraced the truth of the give-to-get principle, I began asking for what I needed and wanted. As soon as I began expecting to receive something whenever I gave, I felt better about myself and my relationships. But I'm not perfect, and I still have to catch myself. Before extending myself, I pause and make sure it feels right. I trust that my subconscious will give me a signal.

This is a principle we all need to be reminded of because we are immersed in a culture that tells us to give selflessly for the good of others. This sacrificial approach to giving is buried deep in our traditions, but for all its good intentions—to show love for God and our fellow human beings—I believe giving as a form of sacrifice often undermines the integrity of the giver . . . and the receiver. In our world, which seems more and more marked by a division between the haves and the have-nots, we often feel there's an imperative to give selflessly—which is actually impossible. That's a misnomer. And I'm not talking about volunteering. There is truth in philanthropy, when you give to others less fortunate who cannot return in kind, but even then, there is a get: feeling good and doing good. Many people will pass a person on the street begging for even the smallest amount of money and say, "I'd give them money if they weren't going to just spend it on booze or drugs." Even that comment denotes give to get. They will give the person money if that person uses it to get something deemed appropriate.

Another form of this kind of giving occurs across religions. From the Bible to the Quran, we are taught that giving what you can—in time, energy, or money—will benefit others as well as yourself. Such gifts, like tithes and offerings to the deities, are contracts with God that you will be blessed—either during this lifetime on earth or in the after-life. Now, this is not to say that I'm not a giver. In fact, I take the act of giving very seriously when it comes to friends and family and of course my husband. I also give way outside my inner circle. As a couple, my husband and I are very philanthropic and mindful about how to give and to whom—which organizations, events, and individuals are most in need of our dollars and our attention and most aligned with our values. I also think of any service transaction as a form of giving and receiving. When you enter a transaction or ask for a service, it's important to offer a fair value for the service. I never try to get someone to do something for less than their highest amount. To me, this is a way to honor that person's highest self and expect them to put their best foot forward. Of course, you would go to a service provider you can afford; this is not about paying more than you can afford. It's about making any transaction fair and equitable for all parties.

Time in gratitude is time well spent. There is a grace in the giving, and also in the receiving.

Ultimately, any form of negotiation—whether it's pistachios for nuclear arms or protection for land use or financing for equity—is a form of give to get. Governments recognize this—that's why we are given tax deductions for charity donations. We get to feel good *and* benefit when we file our taxes—two gets for one give. Feeling good is a valuable and important part of a get. And negotiation is more successful when you recognize the necessity of reciprocity. Think of any negotiation: if you immediately start bargaining, what kind of message are you sending?

Giving purely asks that you understand what's at stake and that you be mindful of the spirit of the give. We don't necessarily want a gift in kind or one that we receive right away. But we do want to be clear that any gift or offering to another has a purpose that is acknowledged by both sides: the giver and the receiver. Again, this awareness is an extension of fairness and cooperation. It's not so much the *what* as the *how* that's important.

Here are some energetic guidelines to keep your subconscious and your conscious mind in alignment as you give to get:

1. Keep yourself from giving to the point of depletion or loss.
2. Expect to get, and make your expectations known.
3. Give judiciously and purely.
4. If you don't feel right about giving, don't give.

Give yourself some time to absorb this principle. I trust that you will find it refreshing and valuable.

On your path to abundance, you will learn that people respect an energy exchange; it signals to others that you are healthy. The principle here is that there is a beneficial exchange in giving to get; this becomes a powerful tool for managing the people in your life so you always get what you want and give less to those who refuse to exchange their energy, just like Mac would have appreciated hearing from Lori. If she had been more tapped into her subconscious, she would have been able to remind him of what mattered to her, instead of standing passive aggressively on the sidelines of her own life. As you consider these elements of give to get and how cooperating, trusting, and playing a fair position can support you as you ask for what you want in life, you may also need to do an active review of your relationships.

Hypnotic Hack: The Giveaway

I created this exercise as a way of determining how your subconscious experiences reciprocity in your varied relationships and to evaluate whether or not your relationships are a fair exchange, or if one of you is overgiving or overasking. You can use this simple three-minute technique any time, with anyone—either for present situations or to review the past.

1. Close your eyes and go within.

2. Imagine an array of valuable, fun, or sentimental/ meaningful gifts. (You might imagine an elegant tie, a soft cashmere scarf or blanket, the latest iPhone or tablet. Perhaps the gifts are more personal—a handmade quilt, a collage of photos, an antique ring.)

3. See an altar overflowing with these gifts.

4. Call upon your SoulSpirit to bring a tone of reverence to the gathering of the gifts.

5. Make a mental list of the people you would ordinarily give a gift to: your spouse or significant other, close family members, friends, or colleagues—you choose, you make the list.

6. Imagine giving one of your prized gifts to each person on the list. Take your time so that you can fully imagine and then experience what it feels like to give the special gift.

This exercise enables you to see if you are giving purely or overgiving. What feeling did you experience giving the gift? If it wasn't joy, then you might be overgiving to a person who has not shown enough reciprocity.

Gifts are meant to be pure. And when you give them, a warm feeling should arise within you immediately. Whether a gift is a thing or an action or sentiment—loyalty, friendship, time, honesty, a shoulder to cry on—giving anything of value should feel good and leave you with a feeling of satisfaction, acknowledgment, and grace.

This exercise also calls upon the subconscious and the SoulSpirit to work in unison. It asks the subconscious to imagine gifts that are personally meaningful to you and to envision on whom you'd like to bestow these gifts. You're also communing with your SoulSpirit to imbue the scene and offering with reverence, by freely transferring your gift to another, bringing that person or persons joy.

You can do this exercise quickly and use it to hone your judgment skills as well as give to get. When you direct your energy toward another individual, the SoulSpirit will reflect back the purity of the gift.

Men and Women Give Differently

At the risk of playing into gender stereotypes, I will offer you an observation about how women and men treat the energetic circle of giving differently. Men in general are much more comfortable with give to get than women are. I have often observed that a group of women having lunch or dinner will struggle with who pays the bill; you can take a fun festive lunch with pastel food and fluffy green salads and turn it into spicy tooth-filled carnage with possible bloodshed—with darting eyes and pterodactyl arms and lots of wallets left at home or in cars, made inexplicably worse when alcohol is involved.

Men, however, trust that it will all even out in the end. They pay in rounds. Perhaps because historically men have functioned as providers, they are more comfortable bringing out their wallets. Women, especially women who don't work or earn their own money, don't typically have this same level of trust that it will all work out. Giving does not require affluence. Indeed, I know plenty of very affluent people who are tied to the get and are challenged to give.

The Crux of Good Manners

As you know, I'm a southern girl who was taught the importance of good manners. *Thank you, ma'am. Yes, sir.* One of the most crucial of these southern takeaways is the handwritten thank-you note. Why this stress on the thank-you note? It's a gesture of acknowledgment and a symbol that says, "Yes, thank you, we received your gift, had a delightful time at your party, appreciate your donation, etc." The acknowledgment *signals the give and sets up a get* . . . sometime in the future. Political figures high up on the chain send handwritten notes; in fact, the more inaccessible these people are, the more likely you are to receive a handwritten note from them. Indeed, Presidents Kennedy, Reagan, and Obama were known for their thoughtful, and sometimes epic, handwritten thank-you notes!

It's expected behavior in the business world to write a personalized email to thank someone for a job or informational interview. You may simply be showing your gratitude for their time and consideration, but it's more than a social nicety; it's a communication to the recipient that you value him or her. And though you might not receive a gesture in return immediately, you are investing in the future of a positive relationship. On the contrary, if the note of appreciation is not received, the other person may make a different judgment call: you don't have the acumen and thoughtfulness to take the time to acknowledge the time spent with him or her.

It's for these reasons that I refer to manners as "musters." For whatever reason, people seem to have let their manners slide; but if you think of them as "musters," you might think twice about skipping these so-called social niceties. These social habits have a purpose beyond being pleasant and courteous: they are an extension of goodwill and energy. That's give to get by definition.

Why and How to Trust Others

When you give to get, it requires that a certain degree of trust is present. Indeed, trust is an important foundation of how give to get actually works. When we talk about trust, keep in mind two things: 1) trust is earned; and 2) it builds over time. Why are these two characteristics so important to your relationship with your subconscious? Because trust doesn't just appear out of thin air. We must consciously cultivate and nurture it. It's precious, it's living, and it's best if it's continual and recurrent. It also reinforces the underlying assumption of the cooperation that's so important to the give-to-get principle of reciprocity.

When trust breaks down with others and undermines the cooperation/synergy in that relationship, your relationship with your own subconscious is negatively affected too.

Did you use appropriate judgment? Were you accountable for how you participated? Are you tuned into your subconscious?

Who do you trust most in your life? Who has broken your trust? Was that relationship salvageable?

Bring to mind a time you felt betrayed in your own life. Think for a moment about how you felt once you experienced this betrayal—whether it was small or big. Did you back away from the relationship?

Did you feel angry? Did you become sad? Did you confront the other person? What warning signals did you ignore? If you get a signal of distrust from someone, in some ways, the why doesn't matter. Think back to the Positive/Negative Charge hack (page 105): is someone eliciting a warm feeling or a cool feeling in you?

How we respond to situations of broken trust says a lot about ourselves, and hearkens back to the principle of judgment. Did you make an error in judgment giving this person your trust? Could you have predicted that he or she was not trustworthy? The following hack can help you use your subconscious to "test the trust" of a relationship.

Hypnotic Hack: Test the Trust

This exercise is designed to provoke an immediate, authentic response from your subconscious about who you trust . . . and who you don't. Bring to mind anyone you consider important to your life right now and see what comes forth from your subconscious when you answer the questions below. You already know the answers to these questions—so go through them to tune into your subconscious and wake it up!

1. Does this person attend to you?
2. Does this person behave as if he or she is more important than you are?
3. Do you feel good about yourself in the presence of this person?
4. Does this person defer to your opinion?
5. Do you feel like you're doing more giving or getting?

   Listen to your inner eight-year-old and what she or he says;

this is your gut reaction to any situation or person. Now bring in your Critical Thinker and review your past dealings with this person. Pay attention to their actions . . . not their words. And finally, tune into your subconscious to decide, with grace and wisdom, what your best move is. Should you change your expectations of the relationship, or simply move on?

It's up to you to let go of the resentments that may have piled up in any kind of relationship after years of not being treated in a reciprocal way. Who does it hurt when you carry around a long list of people who have disappointed you? You. Perhaps your parents come to mind. Or your spouse. Or your best friends. Regardless of who it is, you'll want to recognize those feelings so you can let them go. You probably don't even remember the details; oftentimes we simply remember how we felt.

When you start feeling resentful, it's time to take stock of your give meter and your get meter. Where these are out of balance, you will find yourself depleted of energy and disconnected from your subconscious. This next hack is an important step to readying yourself to play big.

Hypnotic Hack: Give to Get

Achieving your goals and getting what you want does not happen in a vacuum. It requires a give to get, and it also requires the youthful flexibility of your subconscious. This exercise is a useful and effective way to practice authentic give to get when you are asking someone for something—whether that "thing" is tangible or intangible, such as support, their permission, or their feedback.

1. Close your eyes and go within.

2. Imagine the thing you want or want to ask for.

3. If tangible, imagine touching it, rolling around in it, driving it, eating it, or spending it—any use of it that is appropriate. If the thing you want is intangible, imagine the warm or exciting feeling of it.

4. Feel the emotion or enjoyment of what it is or what it can do for you.

5. Now imagine the person you're asking, standing lovingly in front of you.

6. Imagine this person bathed in warm, golden light.

7. Imagine this person enjoying watching you enjoy this thing or situation so much that they almost feel one with you.

8. See this person supportively nodding "yes."

9. See this person signing the contract for you to have what you want.

10. Watch this person raise this contract over their head to the heavens, as if offering it to the universe.

11. Feel the gratitude you have for this event and this gift. Absorb the positive energy coming from your benefactor. Open your eyes. Now approach the person with your request.

When you visualize what it will feel like to receive what it is that you desire, the SoulSpirit bestows a blessing that magnifies your own subconscious power and solidifies a positive connection to all in your orbit. It's this place and position that enable you to ultimately play big.

Playing Big for Real

Your subconscious knows how to stay balanced. It knows the people it can trust, and those who don't deserve that privilege. Your subconscious understands the importance of cooperation, how pitching in, collaborating, and compromising when necessary benefits all. It also knows when to pull back from a relationship or association that is all take and no give.

The reverse is also true: Have you ever been in a relationship where you were given so much that you wanted to withdraw? Or in which you started resisting what the person was trying to give to you? Your unwillingness to participate or take is a loud indicator that this person may not be for you. In an even exchange, you feel clear about giving *and* receiving. The principle of give to get is essential as you move forward in your journey and assume the mantle of truly playing big in your life.

Chapter 7

Principle Six: Play Big

"There is no passion to be found playing small—in settling for a life that is less than the one you are capable of living."

—NELSON MANDELA

You've arrived at the top of your own mountain. You've reached great heights and passed through many a challenging crevasse. You have enacted the principles through regular use of the Hypnotic Hacks and have come into accountability, stayed connected to your subconscious, and become clear on how and when you move toward or away. You continue to practice good judgment and have learned the essence of give to get. Through all these exercises, you now can trust in your subconscious and know how to keep it in sync with your conscious mind. What's left to do?

You are now ready to feel the full pull of the power of your subconscious. You are ready to play big for real.

What Playing Big Looks Like

At fifty-nine years young and after a twenty-year dry spell in her acting career, Helen got a featured role in a Netflix series that has gone viral.

Richard left a fifteen-year career as a dentist to transform his wine-making hobby into a second career—as vintner of his own hundred-acre vineyard.

Colin took his work as a physical trainer and created a ground-breaking wellness brand, authored three books in two years, and launched a line of organic self-care products.

Melanie lost thirty-seven pounds, reversed her type 2 diabetes diagnosis, and discovered that she had created the courage to date again.

What do all these clients have in common? They have used the Power of the Subconscious to achieve their lifelong dreams. That's the essence of Principle Six: learning how to play big in your life so your dreams can become reality. Remember back in chapter 1 when I asked you to call upon your SoulSpirit to be present through the principles of this journey? I believe and trust that your inner divinity has been with you always, and yet now more than ever you are ready to make a big shout-out, because it's time to play big for real. In order to get to this point, you have broken through the barriers of false beliefs, moving always toward what is beneficial, and learning how to use good judgment to finesse your decisions. You have been practicing the give-to-get principle. Together, these form the tools and the know-how to create a course of action that leads to your chosen goal. "Playing big" means stretching yourself beyond what feels comfortable so you can test your mettle and expand your own capacity for growth.

When they hear the phrase "play big," most people think about being the best, acting like a strategic leader, taking action, steam-rolling toward a goal, being the loudest voice in the room, conquering major fears, or taking major risks that pay off. But I want you to think about playing big in a different way. Think of it as similar to creating or listening to a piece of music.

Playing big is much subtler, more nuanced, and more delicate than we realize. Like being transported by music, playing big is allowing yourself to become wholly absorbed in an experience. By listening to your subconscious, you are primed to welcome and interpret the pulse and messages that the universe is offering you. You are on a wave, an energetic wave, taking on the pulse and rhythm of all that you've accomplished enacting the first five principles.

Think about how some of your most indelible memories are evoked by pieces of music. Hearing a simple set of chords or lyrics can instantly transport you back in time to an exact location. At a physical level, music is simply the movement of airwaves; the physical voice or instrument creates an arrangement of atoms that in turn forms sound. It's as if music harnesses the ether and redirects it in such a way that we internalize it and are able to give it meaning. And that meaning is emotion.

While music first touches us through our ears, its impact takes place in your mind, your heart, and your soul. Just like the subconscious, music is not anything you can touch, hold, or confine, but it becomes real because we *feel* it. No one doubts its existence. Listening to or composing music becomes an emotional experience that lays down memories, creates connections, and has the capacity to transport you through time—mind, body, and soul.

In this way, music—listening to it or creating it—is a metaphor for subconscious power, and when you take this final leap of faith and immerse yourself in this power, your dreams, goals, and desires can become real. This is the essence of playing big in your own life.

Playing big is an attitude and a state of mind that helps you to connect to that highest part of yourself, the tenfold of your imagination, for which no wish is too small or too big to accomplish.

Using your newly honed awareness and confidence, you are poised to set your mind to do something and feel the satisfaction of accomplishment. Maybe you want to lose five pounds and instead lose ten. Or you want to quit smoking and discover an exercise routine. Perhaps you have decided to train for a marathon or are ready to take on a triathlon. Or you decide to pursue a new career and return to school after a long hiatus.

How these feats—small and large—are achieved does rely in part on grit, determination, and hard work. It's about moving past previous limitations and achieving that which is most meaningful to you. Playing big, then, also requires a suspension of disbelief, a way of thinking that is less linear and task-oriented and way more immersive. The lens is wider, the picture bigger, and the endgame huge.

Just like all the other principles, playing big requires cooperation and leaning on others. None of us can achieve our goals without the participation, support, and challenges of the people in our lives. And yet playing big needs to start from within and radiate out toward the universe, for you will be calling upon your SoulSpirit to connect to that of the universe. Your subconscious will pull on the power of the universe and invite you to assume your place in it.

This is decidedly delicate work.

It's time to take the giant leap into what Irish poet Seamus Heaney refers to as the *spirit level*!

Where Are You Now?

As you've been working through the principles, you have naturally become more self-aware. You now listen to the whisper of your inner eight-year-old. You trust your conscious mind, the Critical Thinker. You feel more in balance, more self-assured. You've been tuning into your baseline responses to people and situations—moving toward or away appropriately. You know how to bring in judgment, both of yourself and your own actions and to better evaluate your relationships with others. And you're now more familiar with and accepting of how to give to get—in daily life and in the big picture of existence. These principles all lead you to shape an attitude that propels you to play big. Playing big embodies the nexus of *self*-awareness and *other*-awareness. It's the coming together of your heart, mind, and spirit.

Take a moment to write down a list of what you want more of in your life. Put this list aside but keep it handy as you move through this chapter.

Trusting Your Sixth Sense

Robin Leach may have been best known for hosting the syndicated hit TV show *Lifestyles of the Rich and Famous*, featuring the extravagant lives of wealthy entertainers, athletes, and business moguls. His famous outro of "champagne wishes and caviar dreams" would ultimately make him a massive celebrity in his own right. But he and his story are infinitely more interesting than that celebrated role lets on.

In his own life, before his name became synonymous with opulence, Robin had to learn to *play big* to *make it big*. In fact, his is one of the most compelling stories I encountered while researching this book. I was able to interview Robin while writing this book, about a year before his too-early death from the complications of a stroke. His inimitable style and presence in the world moved me to share his story with you, as he related it to me during our conversation.

Robin grew up in England, and always wanted to be a writer. His first job was in Harrow, in northwest London, where he worked for the *Harrow Observer*, a newspaper whose editor practiced a form of baptism by fire when it came to assigning stories to new reporters. The editor simply threw a dart at a map and told Robin, "Where the dart lands, you go. Don't come back until you have a great story!"

So Robin went where the dart landed. As he said, "I was still a kid in short pants and it's raining and I'm on my bike." He arrived at the apartment building and worked his way down from the top floor to the bottom on a whim. When he arrived at the first flat, he knocked on the door and a man answered. Robin remembered thinking how odd it was that a man was at home in the middle of the day. The first question Robin asked was, "Why are you home in the middle of the day and not at an office or working at a factory?" The man replied, "I work at home because I write music," which prompted Robin to ask, "Are you writing anything now?"

The man then described that he was working on a play, *Stop the World – I Want to Get Off*, with Anthony Newley. Robin certainly knew who Anthony Newley was.

It was then and there that Robin realized he was not only going to keep his job, but do well at it—he had found his career.

And by the way, the man Robin met on that first day happened to be Leslie Bricusse, a playwright, lyricist, and composer who wrote not only *Jekyll & Hyde* but also *Willy Wonka & the Chocolate Factory* and many more musicals for Broadway, Hollywood, and the West End. He remained dear friends with Robin until the end of Robin's life.

Looking back on this incident in his life, Robin told me that he believed it was his subconscious that inspired him to choose that first door to knock upon. As he said to me, "Why did I knock on his door? Why did he answer? I don't really know. I believe in the sixth sense. It exists. When you really want something, doors open. Don't take no for an answer. Believe it and you can win. Why some and not others? Because some people believe they can achieve certain things, and some people just say, 'I'm a loser and I can't do it.' It's the hallmark of those at the top . . . they go for it."

It's not a surprise to me that Robin Leach, a man of clear success, had such a strong understanding of his own sixth sense. Indeed, his capacity to listen to his subconscious made a dramatic impact on his life and career. His intuition told him there was a story in that apartment building. He followed his gut, without even realizing it at the time.

The sixth sense is indeed another element of our subconscious. The feeling is a nudge, a hunch, perhaps a light bulb moment, a flicker. The beauty of the subconscious is that it veers us toward what's needed. It's alive and well in all of us, if we listen for it. And the people I mentioned at the beginning of this chapter have similar stories of one distinct moment during which they heard the powerful whisper.

Helen remembers having lunch with a director friend who was describing a new thriller he'd heard Netflix was producing. The starring role was for an older African American woman who'd been a spy during World War II. Helen recalls, "I heard that description and I just knew: that role was mine. I could see myself in costume and on the set. I went home and immediately contacted my agent and said, 'Get me a meeting. I got the part.'"

For ten years, Richard had literally been toiling in his vineyards then returning to his work in dentistry for the rest of the week. One beautiful March day, he lifted his head toward the sky and realized that he'd been waiting. "Waiting for what? I knew in that moment that this work with my hands and my heart was what I wanted to do." He quit his dental practice and has never looked back.

Colin had success as a personal trainer, but he'd thought he needed someone or some company to discover him in order to become successful on a national level. Then, during one of his workouts, leaving a sweaty room of thirty-five people on Spin bikes in the dark, he realized he'd already done the work. He had built his brand; he had developed a loyal following; he had created his own recipes. He could take himself to the next level.

Through hypnosis, Melanie had steadily been losing weight. She'd lost thirty pounds and then reached a plateau. She had seven more pounds to lose to reach her goal weight. I knew that all she needed to do was to reconnect with her subconscious, which enabled her to understand what her body needed to shed the most stubborn, lingering pounds.

Captured in these client stories are not only the achievements they made but also the incredible sense of wonder and possibility that came from connecting with their subconscious and playing big. Playing big in their lives meant success—not by the standards of others, but by their own measurement. And their subconscious, what Robin Leach called his sixth sense, is what helped all of them to ultimately make their dreams a reality.

Hypnotic Hack: Manifest a Goal

1. Close your eyes and go within.
2. Congratulate yourself on all that you've achieved thus far in your life.
3. Bring to mind a goal.
4. Ask your subconscious what is needed to manifest your goal. (For instance, Melanie asked her subconscious to make clear what her body and conscious mind needed in order to shed her final seven pounds. She came to realize that her body needed to rest. She'd been pushing herself too hard for too long. Now she needed to trust that her body would find its set point, her optimal weight.)

5. As the answers appear, imagine yourself implementing them.
6. Visualize yourself accomplishing your goal.
7. Imagine your loved ones around you clapping, cheering, and celebrating your success! Everyone is electrified and glowing with excitement.
8. Absorb and bask in the positive energy from all your supporters.

Drawing on All Six Principles

Cathy, the daughter of one of my clients, has a similar story. In her case, a divorce was the shock to the system that inspired her to play big in her own life. Cathy finally decided to divorce her husband, Mark, after she had caught him having multiple affairs.

Using a mediator, they tried to make things as amicable as possible, and Cathy moved from Los Angeles back to her native New York, where she had family and friends. She was thirty-one years old and had worked as an entry-level film executive. Her soon-to-be former husband was a veterinarian who had just bought his own clinic, sure to be financially successful one day but not at that point of his career. On paper, he was all debt. Why is this detail important? Because when Cathy found herself single again after ten years of marriage, she had $7,600 in her rainy-day account, barely enough for a month's rent and security deposit on her studio apartment sublet on the Lower East Side. Her family and friends all lived uptown, north of 102nd Street on the West Side. She wanted something new, something different, even if it filled her with self-doubt.

At first, Cathy stayed inside, binge-watching television series. She ate ice cream at night and starved herself during the day. She didn't leave the apartment—the roaring city outside was just too big to take on. As she realized that she would soon need to get back to work, she searched for an online coaching session with a hipster career service. She toyed with the idea of a career change and got her résumé in order. She began networking, not from home but at a nearby outpost of the shared office space chain WeWork. Then she began reconnecting with old friends and extended family. She received all sorts of well-meaning advice:

"You need to start dating right away."
"You better find a guy soon—your clock is ticking."
"Get back into film again—you were so good at it."
"You better not wait for your dream job. Take whatever you can get."

As Cathy began to really listen to what these voices were saying, all she heard was fear. The counsel may have been given with good intentions, but instead of seeing Cathy's potential, not to mention the greatness that the universe had in store for her, this advice took a limited view of Cathy and her future. Her birthright was not a marriage to a cheating husband. She didn't need to settle for the first job that came her way or the first man she dated. She knew these well-meaning friends and family were concerned and thought they knew what was best for her, but her subconscious knew better.

At this point, Cathy reached out to me to help her navigate this transition, and I coached her through using the Six Principles of Subconscious Power. Cathy learned how to reconnect with her subconscious and create the life she truly wanted, not the one everyone said she needed:

- She took accountability for the role she had played in the dissolution of her marriage (Principle One).

- She also realized she hadn't been listening to her instincts about Mark in the first place, ignoring the red flags (not showing up, changes in his plans, late nights at work) in his behavior (Principle Two).

- She asked herself if she was mindlessly *moving away* from Mark when she moved to New York or *toward* a better place where she could start over (Principle Three).

- In order to clarify her judgment, she stopped hanging out with friends who projected their fears onto her. She set up an online account with an African American women's business networking website and began to connect with people who had interesting careers in entertainment at interesting companies (Principle Four).

- She hosted an event for women in film on a site, which led to her getting invited to other professional and social events. As she recalled, "I was meeting all sorts of new, cool, interesting people. Then I started to hear from Mark—he said he'd made a mistake and he wanted me back. I'd get five Snapchats a day from him, but I didn't bite" (Principle Five).

- She had used her good judgment and decided that she didn't need to slingshot back to Mark in fear; she felt very clear about letting him go. As she said, "I really felt like I could stand on my own two feet, so I applied as an exec at a start-up music company, was thrilled to get the job, and plan to be here for a long time" (Principle Six).

Playing big means getting out of your comfort zone and pushing past any points of tension or discomfort, whatever they may be. For Cathy, this meant pushing toward her fear of being on her own and not having enough money, realizing that she no longer wanted to stay in a failing relationship. She wanted something more, but she had to do some work before she made her move.

Cathy admitted to me that on some nights she'd go to bed lonely, frustrated, and scared. Was she doing the right thing? Maybe she should go back to Mark. Maybe she should listen to her family and friends. She would close her eyes and fall into tapped-out sleep.

In the morning, she'd wake with solutions like the steam coming off her coffee. She'd feel a renewed sense of commitment to herself and her plan. Her subconscious was working on problem-solving, especially when she was sleeping, to resolve her questions and push her onward in her journey.

Going through that transition presented her with the opportunity to discover how to tap into her subconscious to play big and come into her true self.

The Magic of Restorative Sleep

During the night, when our conscious mind sleeps, our subconscious is alive and well. Neuroscientists refer to sleep as a "resting state" because the brain is still active, even though the conscious mind is not aware. Humans, reptiles, birds, and mammals all demonstrate this capacity for deep brain activity during sleep. It's a deeply healing, restorative state critical to proper functioning of the brain during waking hours, as well as necessary rest for the body. Since the subconscious is so active during sleep, I suggest that my clients take advantage of this subconscious power. If they go to bed with a question or problem that their conscious mind is having trouble resolving or answering, they jot it down on a pad next to them. Often upon waking, they return to their question and find they have an answer, solution, or different, fresh point of view. Try it!

Soar to New Heights

Though I want you to dream big, playing big becomes most meaningful when you apply it to your life in concrete ways. Perhaps you're doing just fine at work, but your marriage is rocky or, worse, smothered like a wet fire. Perhaps you have a loving family back home, but you cannot seem to make any new friends at school. Have you lost your mojo and confidence to the point that you cannot bring yourself to invite a new friend to have a cup of coffee? Maybe you feel like you've alienated everyone at your office—is the tension so bad that you eat lunch alone at your desk? Learning to play big happens on both a day-to-day level and a big-picture life level, but it always counts.

Playing big means taking the initiative and problem-solving, not waiting for others to solve issues for you. In other words, you are not an observer of your own life—you are its greatest participant!

People say "follow your passion," but to me, that can be vague and unhelpful—most people don't really understand what passion is or what they are passionate about. I like to ask different questions: What lights you up? What gets you going? What's your thing? What is meaningful to your life and/or to those you love? Of all your mash-up of qualities—positive and negative—which constellation will lead you to determine what it is you really want? What is your spark, current of energy, or literal plug-in to play big? That's your next step!

You want to zero in on one dimension of your life and use it to play big. Playing big requires taking a long view of your life and deciding what's most important and what's more of a distraction. The following hack can be used to do just that; it's designed to set you free of your daily constraints and earthbound limitations and help you see yourself from a wholly new vantage point.

Hypnotic Hack: Rocket Man

I'm sure you've encountered any number of books that ask you to set goals, establish a schedule, and write a to-do list to help you stay on track toward your goals. My approach is different. This energy for action is inside, in the subconscious.

Instead of getting explicit, I suggest that my clients internalize the entire state of accomplishment they are seeking. So much of what holds us back is the top-down control exerted by your conscious mind. By taming this domineering and often controlling voice and giving validity to your subconscious, you can transport yourself to that place you envision. This hack may seem even a bit silly at first—it's called "Rocket Man," after all. However, I ask that you suspend your disbelief for a moment and play along. The visualization you enact has worked many times, for many people; it can create great momentum for you as you contemplate change.

You're asking yourself to imagine beyond the boundaries. You are in control, and it's your imagination that will propel you forward.

Now it's time to play! Try the following exercise.

1. Close your eyes and go within.
2. Imagine yourself sitting in front of a complex control panel on a rocket ship, and you are the pilot, the astronaut.
3. Your mission is to land on various space stations, which serve as markers for goals you want to achieve. Each goal is aligned with a particular sector in your life, such as career, relationships, children, home, or fitness. These space stations are welcoming you and are experienced as positive targets.
4. As you fire up your engines and adjust the dials on your control panel, you begin to feel the vibrations and power of the rocket. You are controlling the build and sensation as well as its momentum—the roar of the rocket, the sheer force of it.
5. After launch, your first space station is in sight. Visualize the goal you have targeted.
6. You must adjust the controls to land upon it. Make those adjustments real, as needed. Perhaps you need more energy for this goal, or maybe you are too energetic and overshoot your target. If so, back off the thrusters!
7. Once you land at any one of your space stations, enjoy the satisfaction of accomplishing that goal and having landed where you intended.
8. Lock your next space station (or goal) in your sights and fire up your engines once again.

9. Make any necessary adjustments: your rocket GPS, speed, altitude.

10. Then release the brake and begin to feel the thrust of propulsion toward Space Station 2.

11. Repeat steps 1–9 until you visit all your desired space stations, visualizing each goal and experiencing the satisfaction of your accomplishment when you arrive. You are in control. You are the pilot. You know the path to your goals. Enjoy the ride!

When you look back at your stagnant energy from this new position of accomplishment, you may be amazed at your capacity to get what you want. Utilize this exercise any time you feel stuck or lack energy and focus.

Playing big is not a linear activity, and change doesn't always happen overnight. These shifts can happen anytime, now or in the future. The key is to open your mind to a world of greater possibility than you have before, and to stay tuned into your subconscious so that the course to whatever goal you select and focus on will be navigated perfectly, by you.

Making Dreams Come Alive

Here are real people who weren't afraid to play big in their own lives. Their stories can inspire you to play big in your life—think of them as your fellow astronauts.

1. The twenty-five-year-old woman who co-created an app for promoting rap concerts—Claire Bogle, cofounder of ScoreMore Shows
2. The billionaire businesswoman who revolutionized hosiery for the twenty-first-century woman—Sara Blakely, founder of Spanx
3. The college dropout who created one of the world's largest and most influential IT companies—Bill Gates, founder of Microsoft
4. The fashion designer who started sewing her own clothes and ended up creating one of the most iconic fashion houses of all time—Coco Chanel, founder of Chanel
5. The scientist who came up with a cure for polio by injecting himself with the polio virus—Dr. Jonas Salk

Success comes in all sizes and shapes. The person who defines it is the one who creates it. That's what playing big is all about.

Trust in the Universe

Sometimes dramatic circumstances in life become the catalysts for playing big. Pushed into corners, we are confronted with the need to find our own way out of the cave. I am no exception.

If my failed relationship with John taught me how to come into accountability and to use the power of my subconscious to turn around sabotaging patterns of behavior, another situation in my life helped me to finally play big.

I remember it very clearly.

About two years before I met and married my husband, Brad, and settled in Las Vegas, the most important person in my life was my best friend Kelly. Kelly was like family to me; he was the person on whom I most relied. He was a powerful force of nature who attracted interesting, beautiful people to him like bees to honey. We met in a writing class in Los Angeles and became instant friends, spending every day attached at the hip. Soon, Kelly was my go-to person, even more important to me than the man I was dating at the time.

About three years into this intense friendship, I learned that Kelly had been scheming behind my back.

I'll spare you the gory details, but suffice it to say that this rupture had a devastating effect on all aspects of my life—personal, social, and work—at the time. Because Kelly and I were so close, his betrayal hurt me to my core and shattered everything I thought was real and reliable. If I couldn't trust Kelly, could I trust anyone? Then I began to realize that Kelly was turning others against me. I felt like I was caught in a bad teen movie—but it was all real.

Who were these people I had so admired? I began to realize that I had let myself be led by Kelly, giving him such importance that I was barely making decisions for myself. I had abdicated control of my life and clearly was not tapped into my subconscious protector. I was an easy mark for a predatory person like Kelly.

I didn't know who to believe or trust, and felt completely isolated and rejected by my entire social circle.

When you find yourself betrayed in this way, you turn to a trusted friend or family member, but this deep betrayal had shaken my faith in most of my relationships. It was as if a typhoon had swept away the people I thought I knew and replaced them with a rising tide of tainted, toxic water. This water was deeper, darker, and colder than any I'd navigated in the past, and it would require the mother of all life preservers for me to make it back to shore.

But worst of all, I had become so emotionally and physically depleted that I didn't believe I had the resources to save myself. I was at the lowest of the low points in the deepest of the depths. How was I going to keep my head above water, let alone swim back to shore?

It's not uncommon for one huge disappointment to have a ripple effect on the entirety of our lives. I was now untrusting of everyone in my life and withdrew.

As I began to listen to my own inner eight-year-old, that subconscious voice that had been overpowered by Kelly, I realized I had been relying on others so much that my own GPS had been turned off.

Even though I didn't know what I needed at the time, the universe did. It took me away from a group of damaging friends who had become subversively abusive. When it was time to free myself from this toxic mix, the universe presented me with an opportunity to sink or swim. Such big reveals can be terrifying at first, and you don't always feel prepared for the transitions they bring. The sudden loss of friendships, for example, can leave what feels like a gaping hole in your life. Or the death of a family member or spouse. Or the loss of a job. Or an illness. Such monumental events are so powerful, they force a new beginning. Nature's equivalent events are natural disasters: fires, earthquakes, floods, hurricanes, and tornadoes. When we are stripped, we get to such a raw state of pure emotion that we have only two choices: give up or persist. Fear, anger, and an instinctual compulsion to survive propelled me forward. Adrenalin surged through me and I began to hear my subconscious come forth. I went back to basics and learned to swim again. I started with simply treading water, moving on to the breaststroke and then the backstroke. And as my body gained strength, so, too, did my mind. My confidence returned, and I soon felt more ready and poised to make real changes in my life.

The typhoon came through and left me emotionally naked and bereft. But my slate was clean now—fear and adrenalin demanded that I reset myself. I was in receipt of the best gift of my life, one that I would never have chosen for myself or been right-minded enough to know was needed on my own. The rise of the subconscious, the truth, the life that would follow, was revolutionary.

I now know this revelation was a gift from the universe. When such "big reveals" are brought forth to you, you must consider them to be positive offerings, as painful as they may feel at the time. This typhoon was divine in its impact, a cleansing that ultimately lifted me to higher ground. And looking back, as the water receded, I realized that those people had been toxic all along; I just hadn't known it.

So note this: when the universe gives you a message, an opportunity, or a revelation, be open to it, even if it shakes you to your core. In the same way, if you're looking for something to happen in the universe, prepare for it, ask for it, spell it out!

After this event, I was catapulted into a life of new possibilities, populated by a coterie of women and men who were ambitious, had the highest ethical and professional standards, and were driven by excellence and high performance. They represented a variety of careers and were some of the smartest and highly respected people in the world. What originally felt like a tragic loss became all gain for me. My world opened up. My focus became razor sharp as I moved toward the home and career of my dreams. Without realizing it then, I was instigating the principles to escape a life of mediocrity and claim a life of great abundance and success. I had learned to play big once and for all.

Calling All Angels

One of the many wise women who inspired this book and my own work helping people play big in their lives is Marianne Williamson. In fact, one decade ago, Marianne told me that I would write this book. As a world-class visionary, she knew this book you now hold in your hands would emerge. I often refer to her iconic quote from her book *A Return to Love*, and I invite you to ponder it and revisit it as you imagine your boundless future.

> *Our deepest fear is not that we are inadequate. Our deepest fear is that we are powerful beyond measure. It is our light, not our darkness that most frightens us. We ask ourselves, Who am I to be brilliant, gorgeous, talented, fabulous? Actually, who are you not to be? You are a child of God. Your playing small does not serve the world. There is nothing enlightened about shrinking so that other people won't feel insecure around you. We are all meant to shine, as children do. We were born to make manifest the glory of God that is within us. It's not just in some of us; it's in everyone. And as we let our own light shine, we unconsciously give other people permission to do the same. As we are liberated from our own fear, our presence automatically liberates others.*

Love Thyself

As you get in touch with your subconscious and bring it in alignment with your conscious mind, the Six Principles enable you to manage illness, process trauma, and put heartache and unhealthy relationships and habits behind you. (In the second part of the book, we will explore how to address specific issues.)

And yet this emphasis on mending is only one part of what subconscious power can provide. Its other side, the yang to its yin, is all about light and laughter. Remember the story about the tutus? That's the spirit: it's time to dance and sing. It's time, dear friends, to lighten the load, to infuse breath into and revive your magnificent life. This final hack of Principle Six is all about you, for you. It's a way that your subconscious, conscious mind, and SoulSpirit come together in unison to support you as you play big in your life henceforth.

Hypnotic Hack: "Dear Friend"
. . . .

1. Grab a pen and a piece of paper and find a quiet place.
2. Think of a person you *really* admire, the person you admire most.
3. List all the reasons you admire him or her in letter form.
4. Start with "Dear _____."
5. List and/or describe all the person's attributes that you love and appreciate. This letter can be long or short,

but most of all, let this person know what you love most about him or her. (Don't worry, you won't be sending this letter, so feel free to really open up.)

6. Close the letter "With love and respect," and then sign your name.

7. When you are finished writing the letter, cross out the person's name at the top and replace it *with your own* name. Now the letter is addressed to you.

8. Read the letter *out loud* from beginning to end.

On a subconscious level, most of us cannot appreciate or even recognize something deeply in someone else that we do not possess ourselves. This is not narcissism; it's neural wiring. But on the other hand, the depth of appreciation we save for others is rarely that which we extend to ourselves. When reading this appreciation letter out loud, your subconscious is taking in every word. This powerful exercise will help you own all your fantastic, irresistible qualities. Compliments, adoration, and acknowledgment are always appreciated, but you don't have to only give them away to others; make a point of expressing your appreciation for yourself from time to time.

Your Big Life Awaits You

Congratulations. You have done so much loving work for yourself as you've moved through the Six Principles. I just have one more message to send you: love thyself, honor thyself, and trust your subconscious!

In the coming chapters, you will continue to build your subconscious power by training it on everyday challenges and obstacles. Remember to circle back to all that you've learned, returning to the hacks that strengthen and support you. And by all means, have some fun!

2

Mastering Your Best Life

Chapter 8

Respect Your Body

Many of my clients reach out to me for help with physical complaints. No, I am not a doctor, nor do I diagnose symptoms. But I do believe that on some level, the women and men who seek me out understand that their symptoms—aches and pains, trouble sleeping, depression, infertility, anxiety, weight issues, stomach upset, blood pressure, and addiction or substance abuse—can find some relief through hypnosis. And they are right. These are women and men of all ages, backgrounds, and awareness levels, and many come to me as a kind of last resort—they've been to doctors, psychologists, acupuncturists, ministers, or shamans who have offered protocols of all persuasions. But their problems are stubborn, deeply rooted, and often leave them feeling hopeless.

Through our focused work on the subconscious, my clients discover a new way to think about wellness, their bodies, and their physical ailments. I listen, observe, and then guide them to connect with their inner selves, to get to the root of their problem and how they unwittingly may have helped create it. Yes, created. We like to acknowledge all the good things that we create for ourselves, but feel uncomfortable about and resistant to admitting to the problems we create for ourselves. There is something incredibly empowering about recognizing the role you play in your health—once you take ownership of having created the problem, you can then take proactive steps to fix it! This is the lesson you learned in Principle One, "Come into Accountability."

You're probably wondering how a physical issue or ailment can be created, and what the connection is to the subconscious. Through my work, I've come to understand that physical issues can be caused by past or present heartache. Debilitating anxiety can be the aftereffect of a trauma or emotional shock to your overall body-brain system. Frustrated and hopeless, some people don't know about this mind-body connection. It gives me great satisfaction when clients come to me and through our work together, and oftentimes with their physician's assistance, are able to return to excellent health.

What sort of results have I seen? Claire came to see me after almost a year of struggling through menopause symptoms that nothing seemed to alleviate. She used both hypnosis and the "Be Body Aware" and "Body Scan" hacks (pages 160 and 170) to tune into her body and determine if her symptoms were something she might be able to calm down on her own. Once she stopped resisting the hot flashes, moodiness, and trouble sleeping, the symptoms began to settle down. For Claire, her resistance was stoking her hormonal imbalances.

Todd, a client who was being treated for mesothelioma (an aggressive form of lung cancer), came to me after treatment; half the cancerous lung had been cleared by the necessary medical interventions, and his doctors were pleased with the results. Todd wasn't. He wanted to see if he could find a way to communicate with his damaged lung. This is when he sought me out. Through hypnosis and deeper work with his subconscious (he utilized the "This Was Me" and "Root Boost" hacks, as well as the "Be Body Aware" and "Body Scan" hacks on pages 35,

199, 160, and 170, respectively), he was able to feel optimistic, connect to his immune system, and lower his stress. After a month of practicing these Hypnotic Hacks, Todd returned to his oncologist, who was amazed at his improvements. The subconscious can seem almost magical at times.

These reactions to stress and illness can bring relief. However, you do not have to be ill or have a specific disease to benefit from the Six Principles and Hypnotic Hacks I've outlined in this book. Indeed, my work with people teaches them how to use their subconscious to improve their health in general, not to address a specific ailment. I think of our bodies as vessels for all that we are—body, mind, and soul—and they need protection and good care. And when we use our subconscious power to tap into our bodies and its signals, truly listening to what our bodies are telling us, then we are better able to be their stewards and reach or maintain optimal health and wellness.

When Your Ailment Is Working for You

I've seen many clients develop a dependence on their own illness because it "works" for them on an obscure level. This may sound counterintuitive—how can someone's illness work for them?—but think about it for a moment. If someone feels alone or misses a cherished parent, having caring women and men in white lab coats dote on them may fill a void. But what kind of life is that? I guide clients through their dependency by helping them envision their own health and imagine a life of well-being where they become truly accountable. I show them how their illness has come to define them so they can move past it.

This was the case with Robert, who has suffered from a bad back for years. When I first began working with him, he'd complain constantly about his pain. And yet in his regular diatribe, I picked up on a certain note of pride, as he implied that his enduring the physical suffering was an accomplishment.

He described his weekly routine in such a way that it became clear that he was attached to his suffering. For example, he told me that his favorite day of the week was Saturday. When I asked him why, he explained that it was the day he had physical therapy for his back. He described that on his way to PT, he'd fit in time to eat his favorite yogurt, then stop for a latte and then a quick game of mah-jongg in the park. When he got to the PT office, he said, he loved having a quick flirt with the receptionists, enjoying every moment. He described those details with a big smile on his face.

What's wrong with this picture?

Robert's bad back was working for him. He was holding on to this ailment because he'd made it bring him happiness—in the form of lattes, mah-jongg, and frozen treats. He created a day of socializing around his ailment, and that day had become the cornerstone of his weekend. What intrinsic motivation did he have to get better and give up his bad back? On a subconscious level, his bad back isn't bad at all.

In other words, Robert had grown dependent on a physical ailment because it gave him permission to enjoy himself. Through our work together, he was able to clarify the discrepancy between the actual discomfort he experiences in his back and his need for more pleasure. When he was able to be more truthful about his desire for enjoyment and how he mistakenly believed that his back pain prevented him from these pleasures, he was able to use his conscious mind to take some concrete steps to shift his relationship with his bad back. First, he gave himself rewards throughout the week, not reserving them only for Saturdays. Then he took more accountability for the root causes (the tightness in his hips and his weak core muscles, for starters) of the back pain he was experiencing. With these two simple actions, Robert was able to give himself permission to really go after pleasure in his life and to take care of his body in a more complete, conscious way.

Let me share another story. This one is about my client Will, the meat eater. Will loves backyard BBQs, so much so that he even named his grill: he calls her Sue. Will also likes fitness, so it made sense that he would fall in love with Rebecca, his yoga instructor, whom he says looks great in her Down Dog and who is a vegetarian health fanatic.

The two fell madly in love and were soon engaged. Because of his devotion to Rebecca, he follows her lead when she introduces a new health fad—cleanses, boot camps, liquid diets, intermittent fasting— you name it, they tried it. Before the wedding, Rebecca asked Will to go meat-free, and as a sign of his love and good intentions, he agreed. This was not no sex before the wedding day; this was no meat before the wedding day.

Veggies ruled for a while—veggie broccoli steak, veggie jerky, veggie chili. You get the idea. But soon, Will started to not feel well. He'd feel fine all day at work, but as soon as he came home, he'd start to feel sick to his stomach and achy, and would need to go to bed. Rebecca assumed it was his body making the transition from a body built on meat to a healthier body fueled by greens.

But what was really making Will so sick? There was one thing he did not tell Rebecca: he'd been secretly eating meat all along at lunch during the workday. It wasn't really the meat that mattered. It was that meat mattered to Will. Unwittingly, Rebecca had asked Will to give up a very basic but important need in his life, and Will could not really give it up without feeling deeply resentful. But the toll of lying to Rebecca was more powerful than the resentment: it was making him physically sick.

Until Will came into accountability and confessed to Rebecca that he had continued to eat meat, he would continue to feel sick. He was conflicted because he loved both Rebecca and (his grill) Sue. But secrets don't bond us; they shred us.

Will and Rebecca eventually discovered a happy compromise, which allowed Will to eat meat but also participate in Rebecca's meals, eating and enjoying lots of veggies! They both benefited from being more honest about their needs and learned how to create a more mutual give-to-get principle in their relationship. A win-win!

Hypnotic Hack: Be Body Aware

What role are you playing in your illness? The first part of this book taught you to take an honest look at the root of your unhealthy behaviors and patterns. Now you must be willing to explore the emotional ties to your pain or ailments. Be honest when you look at yourself and how certain choices and patterns keep you locked in physical discomfort. Tapping into your subconscious enables you to release physical dependencies that may parade as illnesses. This exercise will enable you to bring into clarity what is physical . . . and what might have unacknowledged or unresolved emotional roots.

1. Close your eyes and go within.
2. Imagine your health.
3. What physical issues or limitations are you experiencing?
4. What secondary benefits are you experiencing by holding on to this condition? (This step requires accountability. We don't want to believe that we are playing a role in limiting ourselves this way; remember, this information isn't coming from your conscious mind, but from your subconscious. You may be unwittingly causing yourself

to feel discomfort as a means of self-protection or self-limitation. Does this ailment keep you from working at a job you don't enjoy anyway? Are you afraid of failure? Maybe this distress gives you the attention you crave from an otherwise distant family member or mate. Are you restricted from enjoyable activities? What is at the core of not being able to hike with your family?)

5. Imagine all the things you would do successfully if this condition or situation were not in your life. In what ways would this new freedom allow you to enjoy your life, spend more time with your loved ones, reach new career heights?

There is a very powerful fact: the decision is yours. Physical conditions can arise from continually ignoring what's really going on. When you tap into your subconscious and really attune yourself to it, you will know what's real and what's not. Yes, you'll have to be brave. Yes, you may need to remind yourself that you are capable and supported. Have faith that you are indeed ready—it's time to elevate your health.

On Louise Hay's Symptom List

In many ways, Louise Hay was the first to identify and define how our minds are connected to our bodies. In her well-recognized Symptom List, which I have adapted here, Hay points to how certain areas of the body and specific symptoms may be related to emotional states or feelings. Consider this list as you begin to tune into your own body.

Acne: Not accepting the self. Dislike of the self.

Addictions: Running from the self. Fear. Not knowing how to love the self.

Allergies: Denying your own power.

Alzheimer's Disease: Refusal to deal with the world as it is. Hopelessness and helplessness. Anger.

Ankle: Inflexibility and guilt. Ankles represent the ability to receive pleasure.

Anxiety: Not trusting the flow and the process of life.

Arthritis: Feeling unloved. Criticism, resentment.

Back Issues: Represents the support of life.

Lower Back Pain: Fear of money or lack of financial support.

Mid-Back Pain: Guilt. Stuck in all that stuff back there. "Get off my back!"

Upper Back Pain: Lack of emotional support. Feeling unloved. Holding back love.

Broken Bones: Rebelling against authority.

Cancer: Deep hurt. Long-standing resentment. Deep secret or grief eating away at the self. Carrying hatreds.

Cholesterol: Clogging the channels of joy. Fear of accepting joy.

Constipation: Incomplete releasing. Holding on to garbage of the past. Guilt over the past. Sometimes stinginess.

Depression: Anger you feel you do not have a right to have. Hopelessness.

Diabetes: Longing for what might have been. A great need to control. Deep sorrow. No sweetness left.

Eczema: Breathtaking antagonism. Mental eruption.

Fatigue: Resistance, boredom. Lack of love for what one does.

Foot Problems: Fear of the future and of not stepping forward in life.

Hands: Hold and handle. Clutch and grip. Grasping and letting go. Caressing. Pinching. All ways of dealing with experiences.

Headaches: Invalidating the self. Self-criticism. Fear.

Heart Attack: Squeezing all the joy out of the heart in favor of money or position. Feeling alone and scared. "I'm not good enough. I don't do enough. I'll never make it."

Heart Problems: Long-standing emotional problems. Lack of joy. Hardening of the heart. Belief in strain and stress.

Hip: Fear of going forward in major decisions. Nothing to move forward to.

Impotence: Sexual pressure, tension, guilt. Social beliefs. Spite against a previous mate. Fear of mother.

Indigestion: Gut-level fear, dread, anxiety. Griping and grunting.

Inflammation: Fear. Seeing red. Inflamed thinking. Anger and frustration about conditions you are looking at in your life.

Insomnia: Fear. Not trusting the process of life. Guilt.

Kidney Stones: Lumps of undissolved anger.

Knee: Represents pride and ego. Stubborn ego and pride. Inability to bend. Fear. Inflexibility. Won't give in.

Legs: Carry us forward in life.

Menopause Problems: Fear of no longer being wanted. Fear of aging. Self-rejection. Not feeling good enough.

Neck: Represents flexibility. The ability to see what's back there. Refusing to see other sides of a question. Stubbornness, inflexibility. Unbending stubbornness.

Osteoporosis: Feeling there is no support left in life. Mental pressures and tightness. Muscles can't stretch. Loss of mental mobility.

Pain: Guilt. Guilt always seeks punishment.

Sinus Problems: Irritation toward one person, someone close.

Sprains: Anger and resistance. Not wanting to move in a certain direction in life.

Stiffness: Rigid, stiff thinking.

Throat (sore): Holding in angry words. Feeling unable to express the self.

Thyroid Gland: Humiliation. "I never get to do what I want to do. When is it going to be my turn?"

Hyperthyroid: Rage at being left out.

Varicose Veins: Standing in a situation you hate. Discouragement. Feeling overworked and overburdened.

Weight Issues: Often represents fear and shows a need for protection. Running away from feelings. Insecurity, self-rejection, and seeking fulfillment.

Wrist: Represents movement and ease.

Where Are You Now?

Take a moment to think about your own body and respond to the questions below:

1. Do you often wake up feeling rested after a night's sleep?
2. Do you have energy for the activities you enjoy?
3. Can you walk up a flight of stairs with ease?
4. Are you able to touch your knees (or maybe your toes!)?
5. Can you raise your arms overhead?
6. Are you able to balance on one leg for any length of time?
7. Do you often find yourself hungry or craving certain foods?
8. Do you go to sleep around the same time each night and stay asleep?
9. Do you enjoy spending active time outdoors?
10. Do you belong to a gym?

If you responded "yes" to most of these questions, then you are more than likely taking good care of your physical health. If you answered "no" to more than three questions, then pay particular attention to the lessons in this chapter.

The Truth Behind Surprising Diagnoses

When you are connected to your subconscious, you are in tune with your body at a cellular level. You are in tune with its ups and downs, its ebbs and flows. You know that the reason you have a headache is because you are dehydrated after a long walk or run. You know that you woke up feeling sluggish because you had one too many glasses of wine, an unhealthy meal, or a too-big dessert the night before. You know that your stress level is a bit higher than usual because you've recently moved offices or homes. In other words, you have an ability to listen to your body and read its cues, which in turn positions you to respond immediately to alleviate the symptom or address the cause. You drink plenty of fluids to reverse dehydration. You rest, avoid sugary foods and beverages, and do a mini cleanse (see page 181) to cleanse your liver and blood to get rid of that hungover feeling. Whatever the issue, you address it so it doesn't have a chance to worsen.

The opposite happens when you're out of sync with your subconscious; it's as if warnings come out of the blue, but do you pay attention? Here is an example from my own life. During a time of enormous stress, when my elderly father was going through some health issues, he turned to me from his hospital bed and said, "Kimberly, what is that bulging bump on your forehead?" I couldn't feel anything, and I figured it was his bad eyesight or a shadow from poor lighting. When I eventually looked in the mirror, sure enough, I saw a big, distended, blue-and-purple vein on my temple. I sent a picture of it to my doctor.

"Be very careful," my doctor told me, "because it's in a precarious position."

"What is it?" I asked in frustration.

"It's probably stress," responded the doctor blithely. I listened. "You're under a lot of stress right now, Kimberly, isn't that so?"

"Yes," I replied.

"And you've been traveling back and forth from Nevada to California to Texas, correct?"

"Yes."

"These kinds of things can appear during stressful times, so I recommend you take a deep breath, sit and relax, and check on it then."

I followed my doctor's advice, and in thirty minutes the bulging vein was gone. I am not worried about it returning because it doesn't have to—I'm now connected to my subconscious and keeping my stress levels in check. Thanks for the literal heads-up.

The surprise is not the actual diagnosis; the surprise is that we are unaware of our bodies and changes to them. When we use our subconscious power to stay tuned into our bodies, its shifts and changes, then it's easier to keep our health in alignment.

However, when your subconscious and your conscious mind are out of balance, you will not look or feel your best. Some people will overextend themselves. Others will stop eating right or eat too much of foods that don't make them feel well. Still others will begin to sleep poorly and the signs of fatigue will show—around the eyes, for instance. Interestingly, friends and loved ones who are in tune with their subconscious will notice this about you right away. Hence their well-meaning comments of "You look tired" or "Are you feeling okay? You don't seem yourself." Since the subconscious is a primal, instinctual kind of knowing that we all share, connecting us at the pack level, we can sense when others in the pack are not at their most fit.

My client Martin is a perfect example. Martin, a world-renowned hairstylist who had also developed a patent for a fabulous line of hair products, came to see me because though he desperately wanted to retire after a career that spanned close to forty years, he just couldn't get himself to walk away from his beauty empire.

At first, we worked through the Six Principles to make sure he was aligned with his subconscious and released any fears he might be harboring related to not working. We also went through a body scan to support his physical stamina and energy before making the momentous change. All seemed okay, and Martin was poised to step back from his company, appointing his second-in-command to take over his duties.

Then Martin got some disheartening news: a tumor had developed around his right arm muscle, the dominant hand that was essential for styling. Though his doctor thought his prognosis was good, Martin was going to have to undergo a biopsy and then more than likely have the tumor removed.

I asked Martin what he really wanted, and without hesitation he said, "I want to stop styling, write my memoir, and hang out at my ranch."

Now he was sincerely telling the truth, but it was almost too late. In response to years of ignoring his subconscious, Martin believed that his body had literally created a condition that would force him to stop working and pursue his dream. He also believed that if he had only listened to the whisper of his subconscious sooner, his body may never have developed the tumor in the first place.

Of course, I explained to Martin that there is no scientific proof for his supposition; but I believe that our subconscious acts like a guardian of our bodies. It points us in the direction of areas that need attention, rest, strengthening, etc. Obviously, the cause of Martin's tumor, which turned out to be benign, is multifactorial, and even his oncologist and

surgeon cannot offer an official explanation. However, what Martin learned from this experience was the importance of paying attention to what his subconscious was telling him. The good news for Martin was that with minor surgery and follow-up "Body Scan" and "Root Boost" hacks (pages 170 and 199), he was able to improve his health *and* finally retire.

If we are disconnected from our subconscious, it will communicate to us in a different way: our bodies will reflect key messages from the subconscious. When we ignore our bodies and these messages, ailments will crop up and surprise us. This is the subconscious demanding to be heard. When we really suppress our subconscious, we can trigger disease.

In the pages ahead, you will learn a lot more about how your body reflects the yearnings of your subconscious. Heed its warnings. Take good care of it. Your physical body and health are an important barometer of the connection between your subconscious and your conscious mind.

Know Your Body

Living our lives necessitates continual healing at a cellular level. Our bodies are always responding and adapting to outside negative influences—environmental stress, pollution, viruses, and a host of microscopic organisms that can negatively affect our bodies and brains. The key for maintaining your subconscious power and using it to protect your health and build your resistance from outside threats is to tap into your body in a regular way. Use the Body Scan hack as a way to do so.

Hypnotic Hack: Body Scan
. . . .

To get a better sense of how your physical ailments may be connected to a non-physical source, try the following exercise:

Consciously notice and write down different body parts that
you feel are malfunctioning now or that you may worry about in the
future. Notice the function for each body part and refer to the list
on pages 162–164. For example, if your hands hurt, what are you
having trouble grasping? If your hips hurt, you might be in need
of balance. The knees represent your pride and ego. Learn to cue
into the emotional roots to physical symptoms. Our body parts correspond and react to our thoughts, and if these thoughts are unat-
tended, the physical problem persists until it awakens our attention.

In this exercise, you will be asking your subconscious to reveal
to you any physical issues and concerns that need to be brought to
your conscious attention. It's not unusual for this exercise to reveal
more than one issue, so have a piece of paper and a pen or pencil
handy so that you can make a list.

A body scan is a tried-and-true exercise recommended by
many practitioners as a way to bring attention to the sensations of
your body and train yourself to attend to its needs. I've adapted
this body scan based on what has worked best for my clients and
myself. It's a great way to connect your subconscious to the areas
of your body that might be out of balance and need some attention, care, and healing.

I love this protocol in conjunction with regular doctor visits
because oftentimes your physician will ask you to identify your
aches, pains, symptoms, or reason for your visit. When you relay
this information to your medical professional, he or she is in a

better position to identify the issues, answer your questions, and respond to your concerns. Remember, a surprise diagnosis can be a diminished link between the subconscious, the conscious mind, and the body (see page 166).

1. Close your eyes and go within.
2. While relaxed, breathe deeply in and out.
3. With each breath, imagine various parts of your body. Begin at the top of your head, moving to your neck, down your spine, into each of your limbs, and ending at your feet (see the list of body parts below).
4. Notice the sensations you encounter and where on your body these sensations occur. (Do you encounter any stiffness? Blockage? Tightness?)
5. If yes, breathe into the affected body part. Feel the rhythm of your breath, massaging any discomfort until that body part feels released.
6. Ask your subconscious to identify the original source of that discomfort. (Oftentimes the name of a person, place, or thing will come into your awareness.) Continue to breathe into the resolution, releasing any residual discomfort.
7. With each new body part, repeat this breathing technique until all symptoms subside:

> Top of head
>
> Forehead
>
> Eyes
>
> Ears
>
> Nose
>
> Mouth

Tongue

Jaw

Neck

Shoulders

Upper chest

Upper back

Center chest

Spine

Arms

Wrists

Hands

Fingers

Abdominal area

Lower back

Pelvis

Buttocks

Legs (quadriceps, hamstrings, glutes)

Knees

Calves

Ankles

Feet

Toes

8. While continuing to breathe deeply, send gratitude to your subconscious for your new awareness and connectivity to your physical body.

Welcome your discoveries, knowing you can check on your body any time you choose. And remember, physical discomfort is meant to get your attention; you can admit nothing gets our attention like discomfort. It's actually your ally, your guide. Use it for what it is: an alarm. This is where the subconscious comes in. In other words, when emotions on the inside are out of step with ecology on the outside, there can be a physical imbalance.

The Importance of Fitness

Why should we care if we are fit? Think about the answer for a minute—why is it important to people in general, and to you in particular? Because you might feel better? Might live longer? You might have an easier life? You might satisfy your ego by looking better? The list can go on and on, but it doesn't matter how you answer the question: it's *your* list!

Your health emerges from the inside out. Getting fit through eating a clean, balanced diet and exercising regularly is not about vanity. It's about building a body that is reliable and resourceful. You know that feeling when you are so tired, your lack of energy keeps you from doing what you want? Respecting your body makes it reliable. Treating your body like the vessel it is also shows your SoulSpirit that you care; this care is a form of respect toward your SoulSpirit.

When I think about health and fitness, I like to envision an airplane pilot seeking balance, keeping both wings parallel to the horizon to level the plane. When the plane lists to one side or a malfunction is detected, lights flash, sirens whine, and occasionally a mechanical voice will repeat a warning to get the pilot's attention. Imagine that the plane is your body and the whirring instrumentation is your subconscious. Some pilots are rated VFR (visual flight rules) when they are new to flying or not yet rated to fly IFR (instrument flight rules). I see VFR pilots as people new to self-help or newbies to energetics or readers newly exploring the power of the subconscious. They rely on what they see rather than relying on their instrumentation to guide them. Until they become experienced with self-help concepts, the miraculous ways of our mind-body connections and the power of the subconscious, they need to see what is in front of them in order to benefit. People more experienced with self-help fly by IFR, relying less on what they see and more on instrumentation. In fact, this pilot can take off, fly to their destination, and land without any visual reference. They are so expertly tuned into their instrumentation, they don't need to have something appear in front of their eyes to react to it.

A 2007 study done by Cornell University professors revealed a surprising statistic: the biggest weight loss or the most weight dropped by women is before their weddings. How do the brides themselves explain the weight loss? Because they want to like how they look in their wedding photos. But the study findings disagree, and instead suggest that the primal directive from the subconscious was suggesting women lose weight so their grooms would believe they had made the best choice in a mate. The research seems to suggest that on a subconscious level we want to be perceived as fit.

In fact, with clients who struggle with their fitness, I found a direct relationship between the amount of unhappiness they experience and the amount of slack they have allowed themselves: the more they cared, the more fit they were; the more slack they gave themselves, the less fit they were . . . and the less happy. The slack they afforded themselves and the level of unhappiness were in direct proportion to each other. In other words, the more they let their health slide and recognized it, the more unhappiness they experienced.

Weight fluctuation is not uncommon during the course of a lifetime, and there are many reasons people put on extra pounds here and there—divorce, stress, sickness, hormone changes, job loss, job gain . . . the list is endless and ever-changing. We are all susceptible to weight and fitness fluctuations during stressful times.

The key is to then right our course. Becoming fit should never involve an endless binge-and-purge cycle. It does not require deprivation or scarcity. Dolly Parton wrote that many years ago when she wanted to lose weight, she would just go out to a restaurant, order a few things, and take a few bites of each dish. She says this strategy enabled her to find her optimal weight and maintain it. She also suggests that she sometimes divides her food in half, then eats only one half and saves the second half for her angels (or her next meal).

Now, at the risk of raising a touchy subject, I want to address the real pain of weight issues: they can be an outward sign that something is unbalanced on the inside. Our bodies are designed to always seek homeostasis, a place of equilibrium for all our physiological processes. Homeostasis is the basis for an interesting and sometimes controversial approach to thinking about stubborn weight issues: set point. First identified in 1982 by nutrition scientists William Bennett and Joel Gurin, set point theory states that a person's body has a predetermined weight range in which it feels most comfortable, which implies that your body will sabotage itself during weight loss by slowing down your metabolism and the rate at which it burns or consumes calories. Regulated by the hypothalamus, this set point also suggests that the internal regulating system of overweight or obese people has become disrupted due to overeating, sedentary lifestyle, and other factors. Of course, set point theory also explains why it's so difficult for people to lose weight and keep it off for good. All our bodies are looking to return to their set point.

People who are either not tapped into their subconscious or whose subconscious and conscious mind are out of sync will tend to not eat enough or to eat past satiety, consuming more food than their bodies can utilize.

The subconscious is preprogrammed to do everything it can to get the body what it needs; sometimes, the conscious mind resists this information. For example, one of my clients, Rachel, told me she wanted to lose weight. When I first met with her and was taking down information about her history, she told me that her husband constantly tells her to put down the chips. While in a trance, I asked her how that made her feel.

"It infuriates me. Sometimes I think I despise him."

It occurred to me that Rachel may just despise her husband enough that she is willing to compromise her own weight loss goals rather than stop eating the chips.

We know that obesity leads to heart attacks, diabetes, and a myriad of illnesses. The science of fitness is well studied; science is showing us that we are becoming heavier and heavier, and more unhealthy. According to an October 2017 data report published by the Centers for Disease Control (CDC), which covered numerous longitudinal studies, the rate of children and adults suffering from obesity or who are grossly overweight has risen sharply in a short amount of time. Indeed, a recent study published in *JAMA* stated that almost 4 in 10 American adults (39.6 percent) over the age of twenty were considered obese in 2015; in 2007, that figure was 33.7 percent. And the American Society for Clinical Nutrition has known since 1979 that obesity and chronic overweight is tied to many health disorders, including cardiovascular disease, diabetes mellitus, gallbladder disease, fatty liver disease, breast cancer and endometriosis, and psychosocial disabilities. These statistics tell us that the unbalanced subconscious and conscious mind may not have shown itself physically yet; but as with all imbalances, the center cannot hold. As pack animals, we tend to judge people who are overweight because the collective subconscious senses their weakness and vulnerability to health issues. It might sound cruel to the conscious mind, and it is. It's a reaction that is hard-wired for survival from our primal instincts.

Some people of course go in the other direction toward fitness and push themselves to an extreme. Sometimes to such an extreme that an injury, stress attack, or exhaustion might occur. Fanaticism in either direction is going to hurt your equilibrium.

True health is the result of first understanding your real thoughts and real reasons for eating and exercising like you do. Do you move away from what's best for you? Do you hang out with other family or friends where eating unhealthily has become your routine and your bond, an excuse not to thrive? Are you in a misery-loves-company relationship with Ben & Jerry's?

Once you explore these questions and tune into your subconscious, you may be surprised at what you may find. At the end of the day, your actual, personal set point is irrelevant; what matters is that you find the real you, the healthiest version of you, whatever size or fitness level that's intended to be. Only a misdirected subconscious is more comfortable in an unhealthy body.

The good news for us is that our subconscious power can alter our set point and guide the body into creating a new normal, a new baseline or range of healthy weight. By tapping into your subconscious and using the hacks that trigger substantive changes, you can adjust your set point. I recommend that my clients practice the following hacks, in this particular order, so that they can create clarity around the optimal weight for them; from this place, they can then use their subconscious power to drive energy toward a new version of themselves, stoke their immune systems (especially the gut), and follow that up with healthy eating and exercise (you will find my advice on eating well and moving well in the pages ahead).

Here are the hacks to use when resetting your set point:

1.　This Was Me (page 35)
2.　Pivot (page 68)
3.　The New You (page 71)
4.　Manifest a Goal (page 135)
5.　Body Scan (page 170)

With your subconscious power, you can not only envision yourself in a new way but also create life-sustaining habits that support sustenance and satiety. You may not consciously know or believe that you can achieve a healthy, fit body with little effort. More important, you can maintain a healthy, balanced physique, because ease equals balance. Dis-ease equals imbalance. Did you ever try to guide a wobbly grocery cart through the store, continually fighting the off-balance wheels? The cart lists to the side and pulls off course, requiring strenuous effort just to roll to the next aisle? The same holds true for a body out of alignment. The fight, the tug, the pull is exhausting and requires such effort just to roll straight ahead. You know the feeling.

The Four Pillars of Self-Care

Your body is a vessel for producing and using energy. It works more efficiently and functions more optimally when it is nourished with clean foods, well-hydrated, given exercise, and refueled with adequate rest. These four pillars of self-care are not new concepts, but they are essential for physical health; they are necessary for using your subconscious to the best of its abilities. Self-care is a major part of playing big in your life. Why? Because playing big insists that you put yourself first and care for your body. Your body and brain are living biochemical organisms that require upkeep, fuel, and lots of TLC. Taking good care of your health is also vital to being able to live an expansive life. Sleep, clean food, and regular movement refresh the connection between your subconscious and your conscious mind.

Remember, the universe will give you more than you can imagine. But to access those oversized goals, you need to be ready to embrace what that means physically—you need to be prepared to perform at a top physical level. This starts with self-care. Have you ever wanted something you didn't have the energy to go get? When my practice began to take off and I had more demands on my time, I had to take extra care to eat clean, take my vitamins, moderate my energy, and get regular physicals and bloodwork. I checked under the hood to make sure my own machine was running at top capacity. I was shoring myself up so I could go the distance and show up for the blessings bestowed upon me. Just like drivers embarking on the Baja 1000, an annual race on the Baja California Peninsula, you've got to physically prepare for all sorts of challenges along the way.

Sleep Well

Your day begins with a good night's sleep. If we don't sleep well, we don't think well. Poor sleep leaves us vulnerable to a host of diseases. It means we cannot be as productive during daylight hours. Think of sleep as the time when your body's mechanics rush in to repair the damage of the day, whatever that is; healing the immune system, cellular repair, neurogenesis, memory consolidation, and more all take place when the body is at rest. Giving your body the necessary care so that it can repair itself is critical for both your short- and long-term health. And as I mentioned earlier, your subconscious is also very busy during sleep; this is the late shift for your body's working mechanisms.

What if you're struggling with disrupted sleep? Remember how the subconscious wakes you up at 3:00 or 4:00 a.m. if you have unfinished business? If you're not sleeping well, keep a pen and paper next to your bed. If you find yourself awake, write down whatever comes to mind. Alternatively, if you are having trouble falling asleep, jot down the questions, doubts, and worries that are keeping you up—oftentimes upon waking, you'll find that your subconscious has figured out solutions.

Eat Well

While I do not subscribe to any one style or approach to eating, I recommend to my clients that they eat as clean as possible. Think of your body like a high-performance car. You would give that car optimum fuel for optimum performance, and clean fuel works best.

What does it meant to "eat clean"? Clean foods are foods that occur in nature and are not altered, including:

- Fresh, locally grown or organic vegetables and legumes
- Fresh, locally grown or organic low-sugar fruit (berries)
- Grass-fed meats
- Wild-caught fish and seafood
- Ancient grains that have not been processed
- Minimal dairy

My Mini Cleanse

All of us occasionally overindulge or otherwise clog up our body's systems with too much of something—food, drink, merriment. When I overindulge and want to do a quick cleanse, I simply drink water with fresh lemon juice squeezed in for a day. I include some berries (about 1/2 cup in the morning and around lunchtime), along with some homemade bone broth to keep my energy in balance. (Bone broth is made from raw chicken or beef bones simmered in water for twenty-four to forty-eight hours—I use my slow cooker for this—after which time the nutritious elements from the bones, including gelatin, calcium, amino acids, collagen, glucosamine, and electrolytes, have been released into the water.) I stay away from hard-to-digest foods and give my system a break. The lemon water acts as a calming influence on the entire body and especially a boost for the natural probiotics in the gut and detox of the liver, which is what gets overtaxed when we overindulge. The bone broth boosts your immune system.

Eating clean also means consuming as little sugar as possible and staying away from packaged, processed foods. Think whole, baked sweet potatoes rather than potato chips. Or a leafy kale salad over a processed energy bar. Eat lean protein in the form of red meat, poultry, and fish. Enjoy organically grown fruits in season so you don't overindulge (fruits contain sugar!). Always include green vegetables with your meals. Consciously include fibrous foods, such as legumes, brown or wild rice, and seeds and nuts. And drink lots of water. All this will keep your blood sugar balanced, help you maintain a healthy weight, reduce inflammation, and help you alleviate the symptoms of and ward off illness and disease.

Having done so myself, I also suggest eliminating processed sugar or foods that turn into sugar in the body as much as possible. The benefits are astounding—and the list continues to grow over time. Studies are now showing that sugar is literally killing us. Indeed, one 2015 study done by researchers at Tufts University and published in the journal *Circulation* found that 184,000 adults around the globe die each year from consumption of sugar-laden drinks. The authors of the study also linked these deaths from sugar to cardiovascular disease, diabetes, and various cancers. The number may seem staggering. Alas, sugar is indeed our enemy, as are other processed foods that contaminate our bodies and put us in such imbalance that we are undermining our very survival.

A number of clients come to me because they struggle with their weight or feel like they cannot control themselves around food. My secret weapon to help these clients lose weight and get healthy is to ritualize their food intake, which helps build a healthful anchor to your eating habits. Creating a ritual around eating brings awareness and soulfulness to the reverential act of feeding oneself. Here are some simple suggestions for creating a ritual around eating:

- Set the table before you sit down.
- Look at the balance of foods on your plate or in your bowl.
- Give thanks that you have food to enjoy.
- Eat slowly, savoring the taste and flavor and texture of the food.

When we assign meaning to things, especially the communion of taking in nutrients, we satisfy the subconscious while we feed our body, mind, and soul. Eight-year-olds love rituals and repetition, which makes this work particularly well for your subconscious: it's easy to repeat the ritual when we eat so many times per day!

Have you been around an unhappy eight-year-old lately? You know the term "hangry"? Giving reverence to food gives it importance beyond just shoveling food into our mouths and satiating our hunger. When I want to bring a sacred aspect to the ritual of eating, I create a "one-bowl" experience: an ancient practice of putting an entire meal— veggies, some clean protein, and a grain—in one bowl and then enjoying it slowly using only my fingers to eat (if you prefer, you can use chopsticks). There are several beneficial aspects to this way of eating. The simple dexterity of the chopsticks slows you down, which allows your level of satiety to keep up with your intake. Eating with your fingers is very primal and reinforces the basic connection to that which fuels you. Food and eating are tactile, and bringing awareness to the ritual of eating enlivens all our senses and literally feeds the subconscious. Many trendy restaurants are now serving this form of one-bowl meal because it works. It's healthy, satisfying, and very close to our nature of collecting.

There are additional benefits to be had from ritualizing your meals. Infusing any act or event with meaning helps you stay present and provides a fuller experience. Instead of mindlessly eating at your desk while working or checking your social media over dinner, add reverence to the experience. You will enjoy your meal more, and it will be more satisfying—physically and spiritually. Even a small change like this to your daily routine—going from mindless meal to mindful ritual—will enable your subconscious mind to create healthful shifts in your body.

Discover the One-Bowl Experience

I discovered the one-bowl concept through Don Gerrard's beautiful book, *One Bowl: A Guide to Eating for Body and Spirit*, and I have used this approach in varying degrees with clients over the years. When we are addicted to food or have phobias associated with too much or too little, I like to remind clients that our bodies are naturally a one-bowl system. Your stomach is your body's one bowl. It would make sense that our outward approach toward health would follow our intake needs; hence, preparing your meals in bowl style reminds the subconscious and the conscious mind to align when selecting our foods.

Choose your feeding vessel. Your bowl will delight your inner eight-year-old. I like pottery and stone, so my bowls are ethnic in nature, collected during my travels. You may prefer crystal, mouth-blown glass, or carved wood.

Ingredients are as endless as the natural food chain. Here are three of my go-to bowls. Simply layer the different food groups one on top of the other, starting with the first ingredient.

Savory Bowl

Protein: Shredded or chopped chicken, pork, lamb, grass-fed beef, egg whites (vegetarians can use chopped avocado or tofu)

Crunch: Celery sticks, raw cauliflower, cucumber, radish

Grains: Farro, ancient grains, wild grains, seeds or nuts

Fluff: Microgreens, sprouts of all kinds (basil, cilantro, broccoli blends)

Drizzle: Safflower mayo, spicy mustard, olive oil, lemon juice

Sweet Bowl

Protein: Grass-fed yogurt, almond butter

Crunch: Chopped apples, berries, cooked sweet potato cubes, pomegranate seeds

Grains: Steel cut oatmeal, nuts, seeds

Fluff: Crisp romaine leaves or celery sticks

Drizzle: Small amount of your favorite protein drink

Soup Bowl

Protein: Bone broth

Crunch: Chopped scallions, celery, broccoli, asparagus

Grains: Legumes, wild rice, ancient grains

Fluff: Wilted leafy greens

Drizzle: Mashed avocado, olive oil

The organization of layering is really about the urgency of the meal. If you are super hungry, on the go, or simply need fuel to move out the door or out of your office, layer your most enjoyable ingredients in the bottom. Chances are, you won't taste your food during the first few minutes, so fluffy greens, steamed veggies, or other fibrous fillers are great to consume while you're packing up your briefcase, finding your keys, and running out the door. Savory chicken, beef, or other flavorful bites are best at the bottom of your bowl, ready to power up your palate once you realize you're actually eating.

You can bring your bowl with you when you are dining out if you like to continue your ritual away from home, or if you travel a lot, like me. I keep mine in my purse in a decorative silk bag. When our meals arrive at a restaurant, I simply layer my meal in my bowl. I might start layering a piece of fish in the bottom, veggies next, and grains on top of that, or do the reverse. And most important to keep in mind: There are no rules. It's your choice, your intake, your result of a guided subconscious. It usually becomes mild entertainment for those dining with us and inevitably launches us into a discussion about cravings, appropriate eating, and reverence. It has literally started a trend.

Move Well

Your body needs to be active in order to remain flexible, stave off illness, restore itself, and offset the inevitable stresses of our daily lives. And did you know that aerobic exercise is the only way of growing new neurons (a process known as neurogenesis)? You get to decide on what type of exercise to do, because the bottom line is, whatever you enjoy, you will do! There is truly something for everyone, so go for what suits you and your lifestyle.

And by all means, utilize the principles of the subconscious to ramp up your self-care:

1. Be accountable about where you are physically. What is your starting point? Are you physically unfit? Are you somewhat fit, with room for improvement?

2. Your higher self knows the fitness level perfect for your needs. Don't push yourself to try an intense spin class if that doesn't feel right. Maybe what you need is a long walk in nature instead. And vice versa.

3. Do you move toward health and fitness or away from fatness and sickness? What is your internal motivator? Remember—it is easier and more powerful to move toward what's positive than away from the negative.

4. Do you have the support of friends and family to take on a healthier mind-set and routine? Surround yourself with doers not talkers, movers not sitters.

5. You are going to give it your all (energy and commitment) in order to get your all (fitness and optimal health).

6. Your fit and healthy body will be your vehicle for your time here. It will support your work and play, your desired lifestyle. You cannot play big unless your body is ready to play big.

We cannot be our best selves—body, mind, spirit—unless our vessel is strong, supple, energetic, and well-tended.

Taking good care of the bodies we inhabit on this earth is a must. I urge you not to let contrast be your teacher. We all know that we only really notice our good health after sickness. But daily care will keep you in your best performance.

What is true on the individual level is also true on the cosmic level. The more connected you are to your food sources—protein, vegetables, grains, fruits, and fats—the purer your connection to the earth and the universe. I've mentioned the ecology of our decisions, the ecology of the people in our lives. Ecology is not just a metaphor: it's the physical science of how life on this planet subsists and evolves. Consider the amount of life contained in one gram of dirt. Consider, too, our basic ecosystems—rain forests, tundra, polar, mountains, temperate forests,

oceans, and grasslands. All these ecosystems are interdependent, relying on one another for food, shelter, and waste removal. From micro-
organisms and insects to plants and soil to animals and humans to air
and water—we all participate in the sustainability of this planet. The
more we respect each and every dimension of this planet, the more
we protect ourselves. This interdependent sustainability is, indeed, the
give-to-get principle in action.

Chapter 9

Get Out of Drought

"I have the world's largest collection of seashells. I keep it on all the beaches of the world . . . perhaps you've seen it."

—STEVEN WRIGHT

Have you ever found yourself stuck in a cycle of negativity, as if the world and your place in it is all "glass half empty"? For whatever reason, you might, even right now, imagine yourself to be the unhappiest person you know. I call this drought. Drought is a condition that happens when you are not in sync with your subconscious; this disconnection leaves you feeling "less than" and lacking in some way. Drought can also be an emotional place or a state of mind; it can be an attitude or a situation in which you've found yourself. And none of us are immune to its vices and vagaries.

Stuck in drought, a perfectly affable person can act like Debi Downer; the usually upbeat person becomes an annoying naysayer, the Doubting Thomas. Like a thief in the night, drought sneaks in and robs us of our balance, our good cheer, our positivity. It steals our energy, makes us feel bad, and drags us down. Drought drains our creativity and confidence and ability to solve our own problems.

Before you think you've turned the page and found yourself in a completely different book, take a deep breath. There is very good news here: drought, for all its stubbornness, is actually not complicated to address. Once again, it's all about connecting to your subconscious and using its power to move out of drought and its false belief in lack and toward all that is empowering, enlivening, and enriching. But it's up to you to rescue yourself.

The tricky thing about drought, however, is that when we're in it, we will consciously and subconsciously find ourselves attracted to destructive energies, as if they are calling us. I call this "pain share." Let's take the average gathering, whether it's a sporting event, dinner party, meeting for coffee, or at the gym. One person mentions an ache, a pain, or some body-part-gone-wrong, and the next person chimes in with an exaggerated degree of that issue. The next interrupts with, "That's nothing!" and goes on to explain how he or she endured many more years of pain and suffering. Pain share literally becomes a contest, and no one is really listening to anyone else, just thinking about how to one-up everyone with a story of the next malady. It's quite remarkable—a sort of pain envy. You know the conversation, and you've probably answered the call yourself, at times.

We may also find ourselves "crutching" on bad habits. Remember how Principle Three helped you move away from those negative habits that hold you back? We can all fall into a cycle of eating too much, drinking too much, watching too much TV, or looking for other empty pleasures. In drought, your subconscious is so buried that you are unable to hear its wisdom and call for health.

When most people arrive at my virtual door, they are in drought. They are reaching out to me because they feel or perceive that nothing is working in their life, or they need little tweaks to get their life back in check. At whatever end of the continuum, people in drought become fixated on the lack in themselves. Why? Because the subconscious is crying out yet goes unheard. As a result, my clients are operating from a place or state of lack. My hope is that they get to me before they become too destructive to themselves and others.

I often think of the source of drought as a leak or a multitude of leaks that are letting good energy slip away. When working with clients, I take steps to help them find the location of the leaks, asking them to close their eyes and let their subconscious reveal the specific locations (for this, they do the "Body Scan" hack; see page 170). Some people reach for illicit drugs or alcohol to numb the discomfort of being in drought. The trouble with this is that numbing simply saves these issues for another day. These substances interfere with your access to your subconscious. Of course, I'm a proponent of any trusted medicine that helps balance someone's biochemistry, like an antidepressant or antianxiety medication when necessary. But ideally, these will be used in conjunction with the exercises in this book for true, lasting change.

The good news? There is nowhere to go but up! There is an abundance of energy, light, health, and good fortune as long as you acknowledge drought (the state of lack or "less than") and pivot toward all that is possible. Just as the horizon appears for all of us as the sun rises and sets, as long as you're positioned to take it in.

Perhaps you're in a job that feels as if it is sucking the literal life out of you; or you are in a relationship that is lopsided and draining. Or perhaps you've not been feeling well—for weeks, months, even years. These are all possible symptoms of drought. I'm going to introduce you to a way to create an "emotional state change," a mind-bender of sorts that moves you from a negative, defeatist mind-set into one that is enlightened, energetic, and endowed with possibilities. Coming into alignment (after being in drought) can feel daunting, so initially this might mean you have to fake it until you make it. You know this feeling already: those days you wake up and you can't even imagine moving, never mind getting out of bed. But then, like a force of nature, you drag yourself into the shower, into clothes, and out the door. By noon, you feel somewhat okay. You did it. This is a form of faking it until you make it—sometimes feeling okay is all that's necessary.

In this chapter, you will be using many of the hacks that you already know to get yourself out of drought. Indeed, for some this might just be an instant fix. For others, it may be a long-term path out of the darkness. You set your own pace. You may not feel great at first, but you will know how to focus on new ways of thinking about yourself, revving yourself up, and pulling yourself out of drought, so that you can plug into a wider knowledge of SoulSpirit-ness, one that speeds you toward an upward trajectory. And keep in mind that drought is really a state of mind, not a state of being, which means it's not forever; it's a moment in time where you feel a sense of lack and that things are not going your way. And it's this lack that we are transforming into abundance.

Where Are You Now?

Are you feeling off your game? Have you been feeling down or paranoid about what others think of you? Can you imagine feeling energetic and ready to make changes, or does the thought of change terrify you or stop you in your tracks? Drought is a trickster and often makes you believe things about yourself that are not true. Getting out of drought means first recognizing that you're in drought, which means that you're lacking in some dimension of your life. Next, it means reconnecting to your inner eight-year-old. Like seeing a child wandering through a busy store alone, aisle after aisle aimlessly looking for something, your subconscious is there, waiting to help you—you've simply lost sight of her for a minute.

Recognizing the Types of Drought

Drought can last a day, a week, a month, or years. Regardless of its duration, it puts a pall over your entire system, blocking the healing, nurturing energy of the subconscious from getting through. A first step is figuring out what kind of drought you're suffering from. I've identified that, in general, there are three types of drought:

- Passing Drought
- Lingering Drought
- Habitual Drought

If you're in Passing Drought, an immediate feeling will come to mind, as well as an immediate cause or trigger—an incident or event—that has somehow undermined your energy and focus. It's distracting you from the whispers of your subconscious, but it has not taken over your week. You just feel "off."

Here are some examples of phrases that you might identify if you're in Passing Drought:

"I had a rough day."
"I don't feel good."
"I feel cranky."

"I'm bloated."

"I pulled an all-nighter last night."

And even if you're not talking out loud, you might text things like *Ughhhhh, Urghhhhhhh, WTH, Geeeeezus*. On the other hand, you might hide and screen your calls.

Lingering Drought is typically characterized by a sense of lack that extends for a distinct period of time. Perhaps you can identify chunks of your life when you felt stuck. Or in the wake of loss or a major disappointment, you felt low or depressed on a daily basis, over a prolonged period of time. Typically, in the midst of a dramatic, life-changing event, we are not in drought; we are in *survival mode*, so our entire system is in overdrive. However, after such events, we can subsequently fall into drought since we are drained or depleted of energy. One of my clients recently described this type of lingering drought after a particularly destructive fire near her Malibu home. She said to me, "We are safe and so are our neighbors, but I can't seem to shake these low-grade depressed feelings. I'm just not myself."

If you're in Lingering Drought, you might use such phrases as:

"I can't do it anymore."

"I have nothing more to give."

"I'm just screwed."

"It's all just too much."

"I don't know what I'm going to do."

"I'm taking my banjo to Mexico."

These phrases tell others that you feel overwhelmed and suggest that you have no sense of agency to change the situation. These feelings of helplessness are classic signs of drought: a mirage of powerlessness that propagates more drought. A note about others: When people are cranky or inappropriately angered by you, to you, or in your presence, it says more about them than it does about you. In other words, when our cup is full enough, we have patience for and sensitivity to others. We engage with others and enjoy our experiences. When we are depleted, we often feel like we have nothing left to give. We have disconnected and might even lash out, inflicting our pain on others. There might as well be a sign on our forehead begging for help. It's natural to feel put off by people who are rude, but if you can recognize this as a sign of drought on their part, try offering kindness for their cup rather than backing away. The slightest drop is a gift and can be just what we need most as we start to pull ourselves out of drought.

Habitual Drought requires a big step back and an objective view of your behaviors. This is when Principle One, "Come into Accountability," will help you enormously. Do you recall the story of Robert, who became so attached to his bad back that he created a ritual around his physical therapy treatments? He represents a good example of someone who was in Habitual Drought because he depended on his ailment to give himself other pleasures. This is a tricky feature of Habitual Drought: it is usually serving a purpose, but one that undermines you.

As you've seen, we can become attached to symptoms, problems, and issues that are no longer true or existing but continue to have a lasting hold on us unless we look under the hood and listen to what our subconscious is telling us. People in Habitual Drought tend to play down all the good in their lives; I call this "awful-izing." Any degree of good is going to get downgraded to awful. We all know that person who listens to your story about summer vacation and only has something negative or bad-natured to say about what you did, who you saw, or where you went. Sometimes we know this person, but oftentimes we are this person. Those stuck in Habitual Drought are tied to their

old stories, not yet willing to summon the energy to rewrite the tired
script; they prefer to hold on to negative false beliefs about what was.

For now, let's take a look at some of the language you might be
using if you are in Habitual Drought:

> "I won't go because last time this or that happened (refer to
> past failed experiences)."
> "I'm sick again—every October I get this flu!"
> "I can't get out of my own way."
> "I'm a magnet, I attract this stuff."
> "You can only try; no one can do it all."
> "Murphy's law: What can go wrong will go wrong."
> "If I had a dime for every time such and such, I'd be rich."

The person in Habitual Drought does not lean to the positive. They
skew to the negative and look for others to validate their point of view.
They negate the solution and amplify the problem. When you're in Habitual Drought, you cannot thrive, and it can feel very hard to get away.
Think of the internal representations in such phrases as:

> "This place is going to be the death of me."
> "This town is not for me, everyone here is . . ."
> "I hate it here, but I have to stay."
> "It's their fault this happened."

Choosing not to let go of your old story weighs on you and separates you not only from your subconscious but also your health.

I first met my friend Terri when we were both eighteen years old
and modeling together. We met in Texas and then went on to model
together in Europe. Right before leaving for Europe, she met and fell

madly in love with Steve. From the get-go, Steve seemed demanding and opportunistic. When we were getting ready to move to Paris, Steve decided to join Terri. While in Paris and later in Milan, Steve followed us, sponging off Terri. To make matters worse, they'd have near-violent arguments. Terri, who was no pushover, would tire of Steve's grifting behavior. Things would come to a head, and then they'd fight and make up in a passionate storm that I unfortunately witnessed, time and time again.

When Terri and I left Europe and settled in Los Angeles, I thought both of us were free of Steve. Terri seemed to blossom. She stopped modeling, took her savings and purchased a small restaurant, and finally seemed to have discovered her own groove. She was happy and healthy in all ways . . . until Steve showed up again.

He convinced Terri to leave California and move to North Carolina near his mother. After six months, they were on the move again. Terri, ever the nimble income-producer, would land on her feet and start a business, sell real estate, or find some other job. But she hated being away from California, she hated the towns that Steve chose, she hated the shady business deals he pressured her into, and she probably hated Steve, as much as she loved him.

They built a pseudo-life together, without actually being together in a relationship. Their life was like a terrible cat-and-mouse chase—it would have been comical if it were not so real.

Finally, she decided to leave Steve for good, sell off all her restaurants and her real estate, and move back to Los Angeles. Unfortunately for Terri, she changed her location, but not her mind-set. Leaving Steve, she thought she was creating a new horizon for herself where she might have found abundance. Unfortunately, instead of moving *toward* new opportunity, she moved *away* from Steve, not having truly come into accountability or clarifying how she participated in the problems of her relationship. As a result, when she arrived in California, her subconscious and her conscious mind were not at all in balance. By this time, she was also suffering physically. At only forty-six years old, she had to get two hip replacements—a true physical sign that she was seeking balance (see Louise Hay's symptom list on page 162). Even though Terri moved to her happy place (LA), she stayed in drought in her mind-set, ruminating about the past, her former restaurants, and Steve. In other words, she did not let go of her old story.

By this time, my effervescent, outgoing friend had become almost reclusive. She wouldn't take phone calls and had lost any sense of optimism, drive, or eagerness for life. She might have thought she was moving toward water, the sunny California shores of which had always brought her so much joy, but then one Thursday when she went in for a regular checkup and routine blood work, she was immediately rushed to the ER. Sadly, she would not leave the hospital alive.

Unbeknownst to her, Terri was experiencing complete and acute liver failure, too fast for even the best doctors to reverse its course. In a mere three days, an otherwise healthy woman would spiral out of control and die a tortuous, slow death. Terri had made it back to her dream spot, but could not find enough wind to loft her sails.

Terri wanted her story to change and thought that she had, in fact, made the changes; in her case, however, she was resisting letting go of her old familiar story. She did not let go of the toxicity of Steve. She did not become accountable to herself and her role in her attachment and negative geographical moves. In the end, her separation from her own subconscious, something that even I as a hypnotherapist and friend could not *force* her to connect to, would be her demise. This is what Habitual Drought looks like when it goes unaddressed.

Whether it's a Passing Drought (like a bad hair day, which I call "hair-nay-do," missing the bus, a fender-bender on the freeway),

Lingering Drought (you're in a funk for a week or so), or Habitual Drought (a chronic negative outlook on life that pulls you down so low that death is literally an option), the treatment is the same: you will use your subconscious to right yourself like a sailboat on choppy seas. You will pull on the energy and teachings of the Six Principles, the hacks you already know, and a powerful new hack, "Root Boost."

Signs You May Be in Drought

1. Your language is negative.
2. You are depressed.
3. It's hard for you to believe in people; you are cynical.
4. You worry a lot.
5. Any humor you have is sarcastic; caustic.
6. You have low or no energy.
7. You're lacking joy.
8. You have continued thoughts of self-harm.
9. You feel like you're against a wall with no one to turn to.
10. Life feels hard.

Hypnotic Hack: Root Boost

Just like plants need to connect to their roots in order to hydrate and nourish themselves, so do we. In order to give more energy to our work, relationships, and goals, we have to get more energy. When we fall into drought, we often feel depleted—both physically and emotionally—of this vital source of motivation and stamina. Regardless of the type of drought you are suffering from, this hack is a powerful way to pull on the restorative, magnetic energy of the earth. Before beginning, find a comfortable place to sit. With your bare feet flat on the ground and your hands palms up and relaxed at your sides, do the following.

1. Close your eyes and go within.

2. Imagine your feet anchored solidly to the earth below.

3. Feel the heavy weight of gravity securing you into the earth. Imagine large roots slowly growing from the bottom of your feet and extending down deep into the soil, then even deeper into the core of the earth.

4. Imagine the earth's strength, balance, power, heat, and energy encompassed within its enormous core.

5. Visualize your roots extending down, accessing the stabilizing energy of the earth's fiery core.

6. Allow the energy field to slowly travel up through your roots and into the bottoms of your feet.

7. Feel the heat gathering in your feet.

8. Allow that heat to radiate through your body, warming the areas in need, energizing any dormant meridians, chakras, muscles, or bones.

9. Notice that this energy is accessible, constant, and renewable.

10. Sit, receive, and collect the abundant energy you are drawing forth.

11. Once you feel warm and full of renewed resources, imagine that you are slowly retracting your roots from the earth's core.

12. Imagine sealing the bottoms of your feet, locking this
new energy in.

Any time you wake feeling a bit blue, fatigued, anguished, or achy, try a quick Root Boost! It will not only strengthen your mind and body, it will reinforce the energetic connections to your subconscious. Do you need a change of scenery? Do you need rest or better sleep habits? Is the food you are eating more depleting than nutritious? Use your quieted mind to let your subconscious speak to you. It will.

Drought Is a Point of View

My husband, Brad, is a funny guy. He's smart and successful, but his humor is what cuts through any proverbial fog in an instant. In the face of all the people complaining about their state of unhappiness, Brad likes to remind me and everyone else who will listen about his theory that *most people are not as unhappy as they think they are.* He feels as though unhappiness has become a pastime, a hobby, a project for most people. Remember the guy who continually complained about how his shoes didn't fit until he met the guy who had no feet? Brad's position is that many just adopt the mindless posture of unhappiness.

I love that. It's so true.

However, it's also true that a normally cheery person can simply get caught in a cycle of negativity; it happens to all of us at some point. When you recognize this negative outlook, I suggest you use the "Emotional State Change" hack to shift your mind-set.

Emotional State Change

The next time you have an important meeting or just want to lift your mood, use this hack to shift your energy from low to high, from depleted to abundant, from negative to positive. Perhaps you have a meaningful appointment or business meeting and you want to show up brimming with positivity and a can-do attitude of accomplishment. Depending on the location of your meeting, you can always find a private spot around a corner, in a stall in the office restroom, or in a courtyard.

1. Close your eyes and go within.

2. Imagine vibrant, energetic, eight-year-old you.

3. Open your eyes and begin to shift from one foot to the other, increasing the energy to a hop. Loosen your body, sway back and forth, stimulating your reflexes and blood flow. (Imagine jamming to your most energetic song. My go-to is "Everybody Dance Now (Gonna Make You Sweat)" by C+C Music Factory.)

4. Lift your arms in the air and wave them from side to side until your entire body is fully engaged.

5. Notice your body is fully and physically energetic and in a positive state.

6. Adjust your clothing and attend your meeting in this "ready for anything" mind-set.

This hack creates evidence of positive energy. That evidence becomes a convincer to you and those who encounter you. The movement creates a brain response of positivity; it effectively brings forth the positive response you are looking for.

Breaking the Cycle

In addition to the "Root Boost" hack (page 199), many of the *Subconscious Power* hacks can catapult you out of drought. Take a look at the list below and consider using any one or a combination of these hacks to address physical ailments, fatigue, emotional annoyances, or bad habits that you now realize are signs of drought:

1. Conscious Awareness (page 31)—Negative self-talk can be a sign of drought.

2. This Was Me (page 35)—Take responsibility for where you are.

3. Cancel, Cancel! (page 48)—Use this hack to reverse negativity.

4. Subconscious Primer (page 52)—Tap into your subconscious so it can protect you.

5. Tonkas and Tutus (page 58)—Call upon your inner eight-year-old to empower you.

6. Pivot (page 68)—Change negative patterns of behaviors or reverse bad habits.

7. The New You (page 71)—Replace negative habits with empowering rituals.

8. Let Go of Fears (page 90)—Fears can keep us stuck in drought; release the fears that block your way.

9. Manifest a Goal (page 135)—Identify a wish or desire to focus on the positive.

10. Dear Friend (page 149)—Loving yourself is an emotional first step to getting out of drought.

Again, drought is not a state of being; it is not fixed, and you do have the power to get out of its clutches. Use any of these hacks to release yourself from the false beliefs of lack and helplessness and return to your subconscious power's capacity to play big.

Social Media Purge

A social media purge can reset your internal wiring. While I'm a friend of social media and its many pleasures and functions, it's important to use it in moderation and not become so attached to it that you upset your own equilibrium and the balance between your subconscious and conscious. That's where a break from social media can help.

When you quit social media cold turkey, the subconscious can rest. This serves as a kind of reset, and we feel safe again to carry on the prime directives of the subconscious. When I initially suggest this break to clients, most say, "Oh, I'm fine, I don't need to do that." That's when I know they need a break from social media the most. And when they do take that break, clients feel an immediate positive effect: they walk taller, their sense of reactiveness is lessened, they're less obsessive, they have a sharper sense of what makes them feel good or bad, and they have more time to enjoy their life.

Move Through Drought

As tough as we'd like to think we are, we are quite complex organisms that can only take temporary abuse from ourselves or others before we invite harm. It's safe to say that we are often our own worst abuser. Just like my friend Terri, who did not pay attention to her subconscious, who ignored the signals that Steve was not to be trusted; that the moves were not good for her; that her business decisions were undermining her best efforts.

The good news is that most of us can and do listen to our subconscious. Leslie is a client who also happens to be a medical doctor and the wife of a prominent film producer. Outwardly healthy, successful, and always cheerful, she was surprised to find herself lying in the hospital with a hernia that was causing acute intestinal issues. After she was released, she came to see me.

"I can't believe I didn't see that coming," she admitted.

She felt she'd been given a warning and now wanted to make sure that nothing like that ever surprised her again. We went through a body scan (see page 170) and some of the other hacks that reinforced her connection to her subconscious, including "Subconscious Primer" (page 52) and "Tonkas and Tutus" (page 58). Then I encouraged her to put aside her extensive medical knowledge and listen to her body from the point of view of the subconscious.

Through our work together, she returned to a moment when she felt her subconscious was screaming for her to stop doing so much. Moving forward, Leslie has used her subconscious on a regular basis to keep her body—and her mind—on an even keel.

Some people enter drought more often than others. But if you find yourself prone to drought, know that you have more control over this than you realize: you are either attracting drought or it is serving some ulterior purpose that your subconscious is trying to help you root out.

Sam is a healthy man from New York who can't get out of his own way. Though he has no specific diagnosis, Sam is in his doctor's office at least once a week. He complains of headaches, arthritis, gallbladder issues, heart palpitations, nerve tingling. His knowledge of the *Merck Manual* is prolific . . . except he's not a doctor, and he's not sick. Sam tells me that he is a hypochondriac.

This behavior is anti-subconscious: the subconscious always wants the person to thrive. So why is he constantly seeking a diagnosis? Sam's dependence on his fleet of doctors and his unending symptoms are providing him with a secondary gain: attention.

When he showed up in my office and his story unfolded, I suggested that he might not be sick, but is actually suffering from drought. Since he has stayed in this state so long, he no longer has any objective awareness of how he is co-creating his aches, pains, and symptoms. His team of frustrated but highly accomplished specialists, full of professionalism and medical knowledge, are giving Sam attention that is more important to him and his ego than embracing his very real health. In Sam's case, he has buried his subconscious so deep and for so long that he can no longer feel what's happening—or, in his case, *not* happening—in his body.

It's also of note that Sam's wife is an avid long-distance runner and cyclist. She literally runs far and fast from Sam and his chronic drought (subconsciously, of course). It is not to say that Sam doesn't have "real" physical issues; he does. Think of it like this: if a smoke alarm alerts you to smoke and you ignore it, the smoke can become a fire, and if the fire isn't dealt with, the sprinkler system engages to extinguish it. But there is no reason for the fire or the flood if the initial alarms are attended to.

Sam was able to get himself out of drought by first doing a body scan (see page 170), followed by the "Dear Friend" and "Root Boost" hacks (pages 149 and 199). However, because his attachment to his phantom illnesses felt so real, I also suggested that he repeat the "New You" exercise (page 71) to transform these negative habits of mind into positive habits of wellness.

When You're Surrounded by Drought

It's best to keep your distance from those who are in drought. That may sound harsh, and it is. But drought can be contagious. It lures you in, just like people with problems they want you to solve. This is especially true if you're an empath, which I'm certain most of you are, or a mother or father for whom nurturing is a core value. I get it. The most wonderful part of you wants to reach out and help, but this is just my point: be clear about the other person's positive or negative charge. If you feel the cold chill of a negative charge, then there's a high likelihood that the person in question is in a drought state.

As I've mentioned, clients typically reach out to me in times of drought, and as a professional, it's my job to help them get out of that state. But it's also my job to stay out of drought myself so I can help them efficiently. How do I do this? By staying closely tapped into my subconscious and paying attention to its signals—through my body and my emotions. I often use the "Positive/Negative Charge" hack (page 105) to assess a person's goodness of fit; I also protect myself by doing the "Saber Sever" hack (page 217) if someone is really in a dark place.

At the same time, I emit positive, health-inspiring energy toward those in drought. I practice the principle of give to get and offer those in drought insight, often using the "Transposition" hack (page 36) to reverse their negative vibe. When your friend is in drought, do not try to carry her out of the desert. You can call her to you. You can suggest that she call upon her SoulSpirit. You can recommend hacks. You can gift her this book. But do not try to bring her out; she will climb onto your back to get out.

In some cases, your friend may simply be too tired to believe you.

If you stay steady, continuing to show her the water, she'll move toward you little by little. Simply carrying her canteens of hope won't sustain her and will tire you because deep down inside, we all do expect something for something.

Always remember that it's okay to give in order to get. Think of helping someone out of drought this way. It's like luring a smart fox out of a cave. You must show the fox something you have so it will abandon all its beliefs about the world it lives in and come toward you for something you have that it wants. If you go in to get your friend, you may not come back out. Remember how misery loves company? Going deep into the cave to "save" your friend in drought is paying misery a visit. Instead, resist the darkness and let your light shine in to draw your friend out of the cave.

Head Toward the Water

I invite you to return to this chapter every time you feel susceptible to drought, either when you're feeling down in the dumps, unusually negative, agitated, upset, in a rut, out of alignment, unable to find your vortex, pissed off, angry, jealous, sad, or when Habitual Drought may be creeping in. Listen to your subconscious, and let it show you the way back to the water.

Chapter 10

Retrofitting Our Relationships

"What counts is what we are, and the way we deepen our relationship with the world and with others, a relationship that can be one of both love for all that exists and of desire for its transformation."

—ITALO CALVINO

Whether or not you believe that we choose our first family, the "tribe" we are born into is the first social structure we encounter and where we begin to learn about ourselves. As you begin to live in the truth of your subconscious power and believe in its power to transform your life, you will want to reflect on all your relationships—from those that are the most intimate, like your immediate family, to those with your outer circle. No matter how deep or superficial, all our relationships reflect back who we are . . . and sometimes who we are not. Living in the light of the truth means making sure that our mates, friendships, bonds, and alliances are ecologically sound and aligned with our truth.

As you know from chapters 5 and 6, our relationships reveal how close or far away we are from our own subconscious. Healthy relationships that embody give to get are built on fairness and reciprocity and are naturally tied to a strong internal connection to the subconscious. On the other hand, relationships that undermine your goals, your health, or your well-being, regardless of how intimate they are, point to a disconnect from your subconscious or a lack of alignment between it and your conscious mind. In this chapter, we are going to go even deeper into the dynamics of your relationships so that you can see them clearly and decide whether they are truly working for you or if you need to make some internal adjustments so that you can retain your subconscious power.

First you will take a look at your place or role in your families. How did your role first emerge? How does it affect you, both positively and negatively? Next you will look at your best and oldest friendships—those formed early in life. These early bonds often offer windows into our subconscious—especially those friendships that began in the spirit of play and fun and are tied to your inner eight-year-old. I also want you to look at your wider alliances—at work, at your kids' school, in your social circles. These associations can be sources of support and encouragement, or they can harbor negative energy that needs to be rooted out.

I will also ask you to look at your most complex, intimate relationship with your spouse or significant other. The exercise in this section applies even if you're not currently in a romantic relationship; we will take a close look at previous relationships through this lens. We all have patterns in our romantic relationships, and exploring these patterns will reveal what may be in the way of your true path.

All this reflection is intended to pinpoint anything that's adversely affecting your connection to your subconscious and otherwise undermining your well-being. To make sure that your subconscious and your conscious mind stay aligned, you need to become aware of the relationships in your life to assess whether they work for you. Do they hold you up or take you down? Expand your universe or narrow your opportunities?

You will learn how to deepen those relationships that boost your confidence and help you connect to community, intimacy, and abundance. You will also learn how to let go of relationships that might be pulling you down or keeping you from your ultimate goals. The easy-to-practice set of exercises not only shows you how to connect more meaningfully with the people in your life but also, on a more practical level, how to make your relationships work better for you.

Where Are You Now?

In the last chapter, we did a deep dive into drought. It goes without saying that we have all felt the depleting doubts of this negative space. Thankfully, as you learned, drought can be reversed once you set your mind to it.

There are other aspects of your life, however, that may need some additional troubleshooting; yes, I'm asking you to return to the realm of your relationships with others. No person is an island. We are all necessarily social creatures. And yet not all our relationships are sound or based on give to get, and some may even upset the equilibrium and alignment of our subconscious. You began to look at this dimension of your life in Principles Three, Four, and Five: "Move Toward or Away," "Judge Thyself and Thy Neighbor," and "Give to Get." Now it's time to take further action.

The Principle of Contrast

As social creatures, we only know ourselves in *contrast* to others. Contrast shapes us. It's the only way we can know what we like, what we don't like, and where we stand within a group. Your intelligence is not a fixed entity but rather a reflection of how intelligent you are in relation to the intelligence of others. Your fitness is also not an absolute, but rather a measurement of how fit you are relative to others' fitness. All our characteristics or facts we think are absolutes are actually relative and changeable. Indeed, knowing ourselves requires seeing ourselves in contrast to the people and the world around us.

This is true on a broad scale—how we are relative to society—but it's especially true when you look at your immediate community and relationships. *How am I doing? How could I be doing? Am I keeping up? Am I accepted?* The answers to these questions become information that you glean from the people in your Inner, Middle, and Outer Circles (see page 213 for descriptions of these three circles). On your journey to tap into your subconscious power, you may discover that certain people do not align with your higher purpose. Think of the people in your life as mirrors that allow you to be more objective about yourself, your behaviors, and the quality of your interactions. For instance, by looking at your relationships, you can clearly discover if:

- You are a leader or follower.
- You are more comfortable in the background, supporting the group, or out in front heading the charge.
- Your friends come to you for laughter, advice, energy, or affirmation.
- Your relationships feel fair and balanced. Do you give more than you get or get more than you give?

How we position ourselves in our relationships and frame them in our lives says as much about who we are as it does about other people.

As you proceed through this chapter and practice the exercises, keep this concept of contrast in mind. It will help you discern the relationships that are good for you from those that might take you off your course.

The Inner, Middle, and Outer Circles

From a bird's-eye view, there are three major categories or levels of people in our lives, based upon how intimate or removed people are to us.

- The Inner Circle is made up of our family of origin, spouse or significant other, best friends, and immediate family. These core relationships are primal and often reflect our orientation toward our subconscious. For good or bad, our parents, siblings, children, spouse, and closest friends reflect the ongoing process of becoming. Some of us separated from our families of origin to define ourselves differently. For others, we remain attached in ways that define meaning in our lives. Making sure these core relationships are healthy for your subconscious is key to playing big in your life.

- The Middle Circle is our wider circle of close friends and the people we work or play with or otherwise spend time with on a daily or weekly basis. These relationships vary in their intensity and degree of emotional closeness; however, because we often see these people every day, these relationships can shape and frame our day-to-day priorities and moods.

- The Outer Circle includes those people who are more on the periphery of our lives but whose associations mean something to us—they belong to the same church or social club; they are members of the same organization or went to the same schools as we did. These relationships may not be emotionally intimate, but they are important to how we want to be perceived by others.

Now that you know the three circles, it's time to evaluate your relationships in each of these circles to clearly assess which relationships are serving you well and which aren't.

1. You probably already have a sense of who occupies each of your circles, just based on the descriptions on page 213. If not, create a list. This list does not have to be complete—and you can always return to this exercise and add or remove people over time. The point isn't to be comprehensive; it is to take a step back and see the circles from a bit of distance.

2. Once you have your list, give each person a classification—Inner, Middle, or Outer. Take a moment to create or revisit your three circles.

3. Next to each name, mark a positive (+) sign or negative (−) sign. This is a quick and easy thought; just jot down whatever immediately comes to mind. This is a simple feeling: Who do you feel positive about? Who do you subconsciously recoil from? Who makes you feel inspired? Who makes you feel bad about yourself? This response is not a conscious or rational decision; it's an automatic judgment. The purpose of doing this

exercise quickly is to rev up your subconscious and let it flow. Be honest. No one but you will see this list. Let the honesty of your subconscious come forward.

This hack also gives you another way to gauge the goodness of fit of people you are meeting for the first time. Your inner eight-year-old knows whose vibe is positive and whose vibe is negative (remember "Positive/Negative Charge," page 105?); then your conscious mind will follow through.

For instance, perhaps your best friend when you were a kid, someone who would answer at any hour if you called, is someone you see infrequently, but an unswerving trust exists between you. This person might be best categorized as "Inner/+" because the degree of trust and love is so deep.

Perhaps your golf buddy or your tennis partner is someone you see regularly, but the relationship is more superficial. I'd probably categorize that relationship as "Middle/+" if you enjoy your time together and stay removed from each other's personal business.

Your boss, whom you see five days a week, may not be your soul brother or sister, but you share a highly important bond, one that has to be nurtured and cared for delicately and with deference. I might categorize such a relationship as "Inner/+." It's Inner because of the frequency and close proximity of the boss figure. However, if your office manager works in four different locations and you see him once a month, then you might categorize him as "Outer/+." If this manager is untrustworthy, however, his designation would become "Outer/-."

This kind of coding will help you clarify both the degree of your attachment and the circumstances of the attachment. Your choice of category also speaks to how your subconscious views this person, as positive or negative.

Once you have spent some time coding your various circles, you may want to look at your main list and then make a separate one of just those people with whom you feel in conflict. And if so, proceed to page 217 and use the "Saber Sever" hack to neutralize or otherwise resolve the conflict.

Where Are You Now?

Another way your subconscious can help clarify the goodness of fit of your relationships is by helping you understand your behavior in a relationship. Here are some questions to guide your understanding:

1. Have you ever felt like your mate or friends don't know who you really are?
2. Do you agree with the mission or voice of your group of friends or coworkers?
3. Are you currently attached to a group that acts in an exclusive way?
4. Can you not function without your morning social media fix, checking in on what everyone was up to in the last twenty-four hours?
5. Has one of the members of your circle succumbed to drought, losing his or her sense of balance and well-being?
6. Alternatively, do you question whether your various circles really have your back?
7. Do you feel that one of your siblings/friends/coworkers is undermining your reputation?

8. Do all the people in your life bring out the truth of you? Does anyone make it difficult to stand in your truth or expect you to posture as someone other than yourself?

Hypnotic Hack: The Saber Sever

How to Detach from Hurtful People

This sacred exercise will free you from people who do not present goodness of fit. This exercise will also free you from the remorse, guilt, grudges, and low-level vengefulness that comes when you break off ties with someone. Not to mention that by taking these sacred steps, you are fortifying yourself against further drought.

1. Close your eyes and go within.
2. With *positive thought language*, call forth this person or persons.
3. Imagine the person's higher-self positioned in front of you. You stand before them, calling upon your highest self.
4. This is a meeting of honor. You are meeting him or her with your highest and best intentions.
5. Inventory the perimeter of your body, focusing on *all* the energetic cords attaching you to this person. Notice specifically where these cords are attached.
6. Imagine you are holding a sacred activated saber (this can be a wand or other instrument that has the ability to cut or sever). You can feel the positive energy pulsing off your saber. You see its vibrant color of your

choosing. (Is your saber protective blue? Searing red? Ethereal purple?)

7. Holding your saber with both hands, samurai-style, imagine sweeping the perimeter of your body to sever the cords above you, beneath you, and to either side of you, wherever these attachments exist, until all have been severed.

8. Visualize this person slowly floating away from you, no longer energetically anchored or attached to you.

9. Send him or her away with a well-intended thought, prayer, or mantra of gratitude for *being* and now *leaving*.

10. Seal your body where the cord attachments were severed with protective light and warmth and healing until all the areas are sealed, healed, and visually undetectable.

This exercise can be used for various purposes and at different times in your life: when you first realize that a strain or tension has come between you and another person, place, or thing (yes, I've used this method to detach from things and places that were no longer good for me); when you become aware that a person, place, or thing is depleting you of your energy and inner resources, getting while not giving; or after you've gone through judgment and determined that a person needs to be released from your Energetic Circle of Influence.

Ghostly Lovers

When our closest relationships are not grounded by our subconscious, they serve alternative purposes for us. I call these "ghostly lovers"—when a person or thing is used emotionally to fill the space (consciously or subconsciously) of someone we would normally give a primary amount of attention to, like a mate.

Ghostly lovers take many forms. Sometimes they are a woman's girlfriends. A woman might find herself spending more time with her friends—going out at night, attending a book club, playing tennis, or working out—at the expense of her relationship with her partner. Her boyfriend, husband, or significant other might utter a complaint, but it falls on deaf ears. She is tied to these friends because they have become her go-to people in terms of sharing emotional intimacies. The relationship with her mate has become more mechanical, while her friendships have become her emotional go-to, her ghostly lovers. She may complain to a girlfriend about her husband, "I *have* to go home and cook him dinner."

Increasingly I have observed large bands of women grouping together and excluding their mates. The problem is that the left-behind male feels like the outcast or third wheel of the female tribe.

One particular case comes to mind. Tim loved to play golf on weekends. After spending long days in the office and many weeks on the road, he looked forward to long hours on the golf course with his buddies. Without realizing it, golf had become his ghostly lover: he preferred playing golf to spending time with his wife. Because he was not in tune with his subconscious, he was unaware that golf was providing him with the pleasure that he might otherwise be creating with his family. Tim remained unaware of his own situation until his wife complained that she felt like golf was his mistress. (You've heard the term "golf widow"?) I'm not saying that golf with his buddies was a problem, until it became a problem for Tim and his wife.

When we worked together, I helped Tim see that he was using golf as a barrier to his most important relationships: those with his family. Tim used a combination of the "Subconscious Primer" and "Root Boost" hacks (pages 52 and 199) to reconnect to his subconscious and get in touch with his real priorities—his wife and his family.

Sometimes ghostly lovers come into play as a form of escape from an unhappy or fractured relationship. When that happens I advise my clients to Come into Accountability: how are they participating in the breakdown in communication? The fracture or injury in the relationship? Typically, clients then go through all the principles and the respective hacks to re-engage in their relationship and infuse it with the light and truth of their subconscious. If, however, a relationship has soured beyond repair, then I often suggest they use the "Saber Sever" hack (page 217) as a way to move on.

Ghostly lovers can be sticky . . . and not in a good way. Take my client Jane, for instance, who was devastated when her loving and powerful father died. For most of her life, Jane's every move had been monitored by her wealthy father, every desire and request fulfilled by him. To say she was spoiled by him and his wealth is a vast understatement. When he died and left her a small fortune, she decided now was the time to meet a man to marry or partner with.

But she dated man after man who would not stick around. It was as if her father were still at the table, the gold standard of all men. He was still wholly present for Jane in her mind. She referred to her father in conversation, comparing him and his wealth to the wealth or relative success of each man she dated. And no one could live up to the memory of him. He was Jane's ghostly lover.

In order for Jane to move on, she needed to let go of her father, mourn his transition and his place in her life, but also create space for a real, flesh-and-blood man with whom she could have a living relationship. Jane needed to return to Principle Three and move away from her father so she could move toward a man who could be a real partner in her life. To accomplish this, she practiced both the "Pivot" exercise and the "Let Go of Fears That Are in Your Way" exercise (pages 68 and 90).

This type of dynamic is quite common. One of my clients comes to mind. Valerie, a young, vibrant, and attractive single mother, recently said to me, "I just don't have time for a man in my life because I'm so busy raising my child."

Clearly, raising a child requires tremendous time and energy, and a lot of diligence, devotion, and attention. However, a happy and mated mother is a balanced mother; a woman with a loving mate teaches the give-to-get principle by example. Of course, this is only true if the mate is truly healthy for her. Women are often too quick to sacrifice their own happiness and become preoccupied by their all-consuming connection to their child (we saw that in chapter 6 in people, especially mothers, who are overgivers). Mothers who lose sight of their own needs operate in a fog of good intention, and we all know where that path leads—depletion, exhaustion, and often resentment. It's often difficult to discern the original cause of these ghostly arrangements: Who neglected whom? Why did one of you turn to people or activity outside the relationship for support or enjoyment? Yes, it's natural for you to find yourself at a point in your life where going home after work to a busy house, a complaining mate, or raucous children does not sound like fun. However, without paying attention to the signals from your subconscious, you might easily spiral out of balance. Again, a healthy relationship is founded upon a healthy connection to the subconscious. When in doubt, use the principles and hacks to resuscitate this positive energy—for yourself, and anyone else you're in a relationship with.

Minding Your Relationships

You can do a lot to control the emotional tenor of your relationships with people you care about, including your mate. For example, if you are constantly texting complaints—the nanny was late; the children are misbehaving; the rowdy dog ran away again—without any positive messages to balance that negativity, those negative messages become a stimulus that signals trouble to the other person. Think about Pavlov's dogs—he trained them to know that when they heard the bell, food was coming soon, so they would salivate with anticipation upon hearing the bell even if no food followed the sound. You're doing the same with your friend, colleague, or partner, except you're training him or her to expect something negative—a complaint, a chore, a criticism. In his or her subconscious, you then become linked to trouble, complaints, negativity. Your identifying ringtone on your mate's phone is literally Pavlov's bell.

Of course, we are all guilty of unloading on a mate when they walk through the door. It happens. But these outbursts need to be the exception, not the rule. Instead, use your subconscious power to sprinkle your conversation with positivity. Here are some of the tips I suggest to clients to create a happy dynamic in a relationship:

- Use the person's name during conversation; this shows you are aware of him or her. Personalizing conversation deepens rapport.
- Ask questions; this shows that you are interested in the other person.

- Add positive inflections, such as "Wonderful," "Wow," "That's so interesting," a technique I learned from one of my mentors, Shelley Stockwell-Nicholas. Everyone appreciates positive feedback.
- If you're together face-to-face, engage in eye contact.
- Touch signifies closeness; be receptive to touch as well.
- Listen to what your partner has to say.

Unresolved Issues

Some people who figure in your Energetic Circle of Influence might have passed on (or, as I like to say, transitioned). You may still feel close to and share a loving bond with this person, in which case they would be categorized as "Inner/+"). (In the next chapter, we will explore relationships with people who are no longer physically present.)

One of my clients shared a story about how, despite the fact that she was happily married with two kids, three dogs, and a cat, she would often go on Facebook at night, trolling for information about a childhood mentor who had coached her as a competitive swimmer throughout her time during high school and college. The relationship ended dramatically when her coach moved suddenly. The dean announced that the swim coach would not be returning. This event was so traumatic for her that she quit swimming, never to compete again. But now, twenty years later, a sense of irresolution keeps her bonded to him even though she has grown and, for all practical purposes, moved on.

When I asked her to categorize this man, her subconscious chose "Inner/–." The fact that she categorized him as "Inner" indicates how "present" the relationship still was for her. In order to resolve her feelings, I explained that she needed to return to the first principle and come into accountability—how and why was she still attached to the story that her coach had "left" her when he moved out of state? She used the "This Was Me" hack (page 35) to acknowledge how important the coach had been to her sense of safety at that time in her life. She was able to understand that he, even more than her own family, gave her a sense of security as a teenager. Next she was able to acknowledge that she was not that same teenager any longer; she had her own husband and family. She was indeed safe and secure, even without the coach's presence. This shift enabled her to come to peace with the fact that he had moved.

It's very common to fixate on relationships that feel unresolved. Coding your relationships can bring a certain clarity to whether they are currently working for you. In the case of this client, she was finally able to accept all that she had given to swimming and to recast her feelings about her former coach as positive, and move on.

The Six Principles and Your Circle of Influence

Now that you have gained more insight into who is in your life and the charge of each of those relationships, it's time to use the Six Principles to evaluate the health or ecology of these people. You may want to start with your Inner Circle, but you can use this exercise for every person in your life. In this exercise, you will mindfully go through each step, allowing your subconscious to guide you.

1. Come into Accountability: In using the Six Principles for evaluating the health of your relationships, we began with your coding the emotion and the position of each person. In that

exercise, your subconscious enabled you to come into accountability with the other person.

2. Tap into Your Subconscious: Now close your eyes and go within, connecting with your subconscious, and ask:

    - Does your subconscious trust this person?
    - How does your subconscious recognize his or her energy?
    - What does your conscious mind know about this person's patterns and behaviors?

3. Move Toward or Away: The third step is to let your subconscious reveal whether you are moving toward this person or backing away from this person.

4. Judge Thyself and Thy Neighbor. When you utilize the tools of nonverbal expression, what signals do you pick up about this person? How does your subconscious judge his or her goodness of fit, or discern whether he or she is to be trusted? Do you feel any fear or apprehension?

5. Give to Get: Now it's time to evaluate whether the relationship is based on fairness and reciprocity.

    - Do you each give to the relationship equally?
    - Is one of you more dependent on the other?
    - Is one of you more loving than the other?
    - Has the dynamic been tainted by unequal transaction or bolstered by fairness and mutual support?

6.　Play Big: Finally, you are ready to decide if the relationship in question allows you to play big in your life. Tap into your subconscious to answer:

- Does this person boost your confidence?
- Does this person make you feel good about yourself?
- Does this person doubt your abilities?
- Does this person keep you tethered to past failures or mistakes?

This exercise of applying the Six Principles to your relationships may feel uncomfortable. I get it. However, chances are the relationships may be more uncomfortable than the realizations. This task can awaken some surprising and enlightening insights. The key is to remember that you chose these people and these relationships at some time, on some level. That means you're in control of whether they continue in your life or not. Answering these questions honestly and openly will enable you to free your true self and cultivate only the relationships you truly want.

Our Relationships Deepen Our World

We cannot live alone. Without question, our relationships form the texture of our lives—the place where we experience love and laughter, purpose and pride, energy and drive, and, yes, sometimes loss, frustration, and betrayal. However, when we bring our subconscious awareness to our relationships—present, past, and future—we give ourselves an amazing opportunity to clarify who we are and what we want to achieve in this lifetime.

3

Leap of Faith

Chapter 11

Life Is a Loop, Not a Line

"You live on earth only for a few short years, which you call an incarnation, and then you leave your body as an outworn dress and go for refreshment to your true home in the spirit."

—WHITE EAGLE, NATIVE AMERICAN
SPIRITUAL TEACHER

My friend Kiki Tyson and I are so close, we are connected at the level of the SoulSpirit. Our closeness is not dependent on being together in person. We attune to each other simply when one of us thinks of the other. A second later, one of our phones will ring.

Has this ever happened to you?

Many people I know experience this kind of deep connection with friends or family—a connection I think of as deeply tied to our subconscious. Kiki is, like me, deeply rooted in her instincts and intuition; she is also married to one of the most primal men the world has ever known, the undisputed world heavyweight champion, Mike Tyson.

One particular time when I called Kiki, she was preparing for Muhammad Ali's funeral service. The great fighter, civil rights advocate, and humanitarian had died at age seventy-four, and a celebration of his life and a funeral were to take place in his hometown of Louisville, Kentucky, on June 10, 2016. Kiki's husband, Mike, had been asked to serve Muhammad one final time as a pallbearer. She explained that Mike couldn't possibly be in Kentucky in time to serve as pallbearer because most private jets in Las Vegas were already booked.

On the phone, Kiki reminded me that Mike was performing in his sold-out show "The Undisputed Truth" in Las Vegas. She explained that there was "no way" they could make the air travel schedule work and still get back in time for Mike to meet his obligation to fans and ticketholders. Mike wouldn't be able to accept the honor of a lifetime and carry Muhammad Ali to his final resting spot. They were devastated. Both Kiki and Mike revered Ali, and couldn't imagine missing this great honor and showing their respect to him and his family.

When I heard the words "no way," I immediately thought of something Philippe Petit (the famous high-wire walker of *The Walk* and *Man on Wire*, who tightrope walked across a steel cable strung between the Twin Towers in 1974) had once told me: "The most likely answer to any complex issue is the most simple, elegant one." This tool of stripping down problems to their most basic parts is one of the fundamental reasons Petit himself is still alive. Though his high-wire miracles involve engineering, thermodynamics, physics, and incredible athleticism, Petit does not focus on the stunt's complexity. Instead he drills down to its simple center. For me, this is a metaphor for one of the many outcomes of believing in the power of the SoulSpirit, that spiritual or divine connection we all have inside of us.

Before I could even finish my call with Kiki, I was already thinking of how I could get them to Kentucky for the funeral and back in time for Mike to make his call time in Vegas.

Muhammad Ali's funeral was a historic send-off, with billions of people watching. Many religious, political, and athletic luminaries paid homage to him. Religious leaders of all faiths gave moving speeches about his commitment to civil rights. President Bill Clinton spoke, as did Senator Orrin Hatch and comedian Billy Crystal. President Obama offered his condolences in a written statement, and Muhammad's widow, Lonnie, delivered one of the most moving eulogies of the event:

> If Muhammad didn't like the rules, he rewrote them. His religion, his beliefs, his name were his to fashion, no matter what the cost. Muhammad wants young people of every background to see his life as proof that adversity can make you stronger. It cannot rob you of the power to dream, and to reach your dreams.

To say that Muhammad Ali knew how to play big in his life is an understatement.

Fittingly, Mike Tyson as pallbearer was at this historic event to honor his dear friend's memory.

After the funeral, Mike and Kiki returned to Vegas so Mike could do his show, and I called the friend who had helped arrange for the Tysons' flight to thank her. She knew that all of us—Kiki, Mike, and I—were grateful for her intervention at such an important time.

My friend was glad to help out. And then she said something surprising: "Wow, I bet Mike is really impressed with you."

I laughed and said, "I wasn't looking to impress Mike—I was looking to impress Muhammad!"

Yes, I had met the great Muhammad Ali a few times in person toward the end of his life. He was indeed impressive, an imposing figure even in his twilight. But what I meant in this moment was related to my faith that I could help my friends. In the big picture, helping them access a private jet was not such a big deal. It was helping them get to an event that had so much spiritual importance to them and to the world—and that mattered to me. In fact, I didn't find them that private jet; the SoulSpirit worked through me to find it. The realm of the SoulSpirit is useful, creative, and intentional. Actions and events done in spirit roll out as intended. If this included me in some small way, that's an honor. And yet I know that I was only a small conduit in the greater workings of the SoulSpirit.

I share this particular story because it's a very good example of the SoulSpirit at work in various ways. No doubt, you have picked up on some of them: my SoulSpirit connection with Kiki; my using give to get to arrange the private jet; and the synergy of all of it taking place so fluidly. Underneath all these acts, a crystallization of purpose occurred: when we move on from this planet, the universe widens and opens to allow energy to flow through. I am a firm believer that we remain connected to our loved ones even when they have transitioned. This is why funeral services can feel so healing and cathartic. It's why we work so hard to show up even though the timing is almost always inconvenient.

And the SoulSpirit is always there, waiting to help us, to guide us, to bring us into a realm where anything is possible. This is just one of a thousand stories of the power of the energetic loop.

Communing with the SoulSpirit

Ultimately, the point of this story is that life is not a line; it's a loop— not exclusive but inclusive; not solid but vibrational. It offers us an opportunity to connect to all the people who come into and out of our lives, knowing their souls are still living, energetic entities.

When my clients are willing to take this leap of faith in our sessions, they experience a level of hyperawareness that has allowed them to feel truly connected to the universe. One client was able to connect with her unborn child. Another was able to connect with her favorite dog, who had transitioned. Still another client was able to repair a tattered relationship with his deceased father, finding peace after many years of living with rancor.

I've waited to share this concept until the end of the book, when you have had time to experience your own energetic connections in the universe. I trust that you now know how to tap into your subconscious and use its wisdom—both practical and profound—to shift your attitude out of drought, to heal relationships, and to live healthier. I trust that you have become more truthful with yourself and others, and you have learned and acted upon the truth of give to get and used your own good judgment to steer your life's trajectory. If you are able to tap into your true subconscious power, using all Six Principles, then that is a sign that you are ready to connect to the larger universe, outside of time.

You are ready to understand that life is a loop, not a line. And this loop cannot be broken.

Regardless of your religious or spiritual beliefs, we can all agree about the timeless nature of the universe, the interconnectedness of people through and across time. And now it's your time.

This concept is familiar across different religious and traditions: Eastern Indians refer to it as *prana*; the Chinese call this energy chi; Westerners refer to the soul. Buddhist and Christian monks have understood how meditative practice opens the full power of the mind to attend, focus, and calm.

However you conceive of this power that transcends time and unites us all is up to you. But I ask you to believe in its presence and its power.

Pulling on the Power

For many of us who call upon those who have transitioned, the departed can be a source of support, guidance, and enduring love. Why,

I ask, would one give that up? When you embrace life as a loop, not a line, you simply open doors to more energy, succor, and guidance from those in high places.

Here's a powerful story, told to me by a colleague Brigitte about an experience she shared with her husband, Leonard. As a married couple in their forties, they had recently bought a guest ranch in New Mexico, 220 miles from El Paso. Their son, Jeff, went to the regional high school. Jeff was incredibly helpful on the ranch, and he worked hard during the week. One Friday night, Jeff asked if he could borrow the pickup truck to meet up with some of his buddies at a school basketball game.

He never came back. On his way home during a heavy rainstorm, he skidded off the dark mountain road.

Brigitte and Leonard were devastated, gutted to the core, and could not leave their ranch, no matter how many well-wishers reached out to them with their condolences. Leonard could not work. Brigitte could not eat. Jeff had been the center of their life. They couldn't stop thinking about and imagining the pain and terror Jeff must have experienced during the accident. Jeff was such a hard worker; it was their greatest pleasure to let him go to the game that night. But what was supposed to be a fun night out for Jeff turned into his last. Leonard and Brigitte circled that idea over and over again, ruminating on it.

One evening, several months after Jeff had passed, there was a knock on the front door of the guest ranch. A well-dressed man said he was a driver for a lady, and he wondered if the lady might come in and use their restroom and have some refreshments.

"Of course," Leonard said, without hesitation.

The man turned back to the car and then escorted an impeccably dressed woman up the front steps.

Brigitte and Leonard waited in the foyer ready to greet the woman and her driver. The woman was wearing a hat and a long, sumptuous coat. She looked up at them and Leonard and Brigitte gasped. The woman was none other than the beautiful Shirley MacLaine.

Speaking solemnly, Ms. MacLaine said that something very powerful had happened there. As she was driving by, she saw a cote of white doves circling their home and felt compelled to stop in. "The doves have a message for you," she said, and then explained that their son wanted them to know he was all right. "He's here to tell you he's fine and he's sending love to you both."

Brigitte and Leonard knew that Shirley MacLaine was a highly spiritual person, but it was still remarkable to have her standing there, relaying this healing message from their son. Neither Brigitte nor Leonard would identify as spiritual people; they were more pragmatic by nature. However, they were overwhelmed with the feeling of assurance that their son's energy was still with them, despite this horrific accident.

In between sips of tea, it became clear that Ms. MacLaine's decision to stop at the ranch was an intentional act of great generosity on her part; her stopping was no coincidence. After her visit, Brigitte and Leonard felt better. They were able to let go of their physical suffering and mourning and began to reenter their lives. Although they will never go a day without missing Jeffrey, they feel tremendous relief knowing that their sweet son was "all right" and not in pain and, though no longer physically present, he was still with them.

This story gives an exceptional glimpse into how the SoulSpirit can work, but it also portrays give to get: Brigitte and Leonard opened their door to a woman who needed a rest while on a long journey, and she gave them something invaluable in return. Both parties were on long journeys, one physical and one spiritual.

No one of us knows for certain what happens when our physical bodies die. The only thing we do know and can control is our perception of what happens when someone we love transitions.

If you've ever been in the presence of a dying person, you can feel their soul abandoning its shell. It's a good thing Benjamin Franklin chose to be a believer in energy he could feel but could not see. I also believe we will one day capture the energy that has left the physical body, but for now, this is how you, too, can enjoy the company of those you love and respect, even though they have transitioned. Trusting in your ability to stay in touch through the power of the SoulSpirit and your own subconscious offers you that succor.

Your Angels Above

I regularly receive and reach out for messages from my friends and family who have transitioned. I believe that most of the time, this information is helpful and will offer insight for life in this dimension. A dear departed friend, Emilie, visited me in my dreams one night and conveyed that she was worried about my heart. I visualize my friends who have transitioned as angels, and I frequently call on them to deliver a more nuanced kind of insight and truth, such as a level of knowledge that is not yet clear to the rest of us. At the time of her passing, Emilie was seemingly healthy, but died quickly and unexpectedly. In my dream, Emilie implied that she wanted me to have my heart checked. I'm one of the healthiest people I know, so I was surprised by this message. And so was my doctor when I asked him to check my heart; he saw no medical reason to do so. But in my world, if an angel friend gives me a message, I'm going to listen to it.

Sure enough, after a test or two, I landed in a cardiac surgeon's office to discuss a mass found on my heart's lining. I was officially diagnosed with a pericardial cyst—a benign cyst, thankfully, but one that would require observation. Remember in chapter 8, when we learned about the ways the body speaks to us through illness? According to well-regarded mind-body theorists such as Louise Hay and Candace Pert, cysts represent false beliefs that no longer serve us. Pericardial cysts are very rare and rarely discovered and I was fortunate to have been alerted to it. *Thanks, Emilie!*

Of course, the doctors were more than intrigued when I gave full credit to Emilie and my dream for helping to find the cyst. They had run the tests to appease me and were honestly surprised to find anything at all. I told my doctors I would put in a good word with my angel Emilie and perhaps she'd watch over their physical bodies, too.

Sometimes what we need to heal or address isn't apparent to us or to highly trained medical professionals. When this happens, your subconscious and your SoulSpirit can bring it to our conscious awareness, just like my angel friend Emilie did for me. It's important to share these insights or angel alerts with your doctor.

Connecting to the SoulSpirit energy may take a bit of getting used to. If your beliefs are solely rooted in the physical, you might also expect your conscious mind (your Critical Thinker) to voice a bit of suspicion or doubt. Your inner eight-year-old, of course, knows better. All that I suggest now is staying open: a lot of valuable information can transmit if you're willing to be receptive and "go there."

Hypnotic Hack: Making Contact

People may be out of sight, but that doesn't mean they are out of insight or out of reach. Is there someone you'd like to speak to again? Here is how to get the attention of your friends and family, on the other side:

1. Close your eyes and go within.

2. Imagine your loved one at one of their happiest times.

3. Visualize them noticing you and ask their higher self to come and connect with your higher self.

4. Imagine them in detail—how they look, smell, sound, and feel.

5. Commune with them in an activity that you both enjoyed while they were on earth. Did you both enjoy baking? Taking walks? Going to the movies? Imagine that you are spending some time in this activity with them.

6. Let them know with thought language how much you appreciate them visiting you.

7. Let them know that you enjoy spending time with them, and invite them to visit as often as they are comfortable doing so.

8. Let them know you think of them often and will be watching for signals from them.

9. Thank them for showing up for you.

In addition to inviting your departed loved ones to visit, it's very important to be aware when they do appear. The soul energy from a loved one can appear in natural archetypal ways: hummingbirds, butterflies, rainbows, clouds, or any animal or creature you associate with that person. Soul energy can appear through energetic sources and conduits like media equipment, water, musical instruments, electrical appliances, lights, and, of course, dreams. You may dream of this person or wake up to an aroma or scent that reminds you of them. Sometimes it's easier for them to reach us when we are dreaming and not consciously aware. When we are sleeping, we are less critically minded and more tuned into our subconscious, which makes us more open to things that don't make logical sense. It's easier for energy to move when it's not resisted.

It is said we die twice: once with our physical bodies and then the last time anyone says our name. So call your transitioned loved ones by name. I say hi to Emilie (and other dear friends) in the morning, and I blow her a kiss at night. I thank her for her guidance, and I ask her to alert me to anything I may need to know. I also ask a few other angel girlfriends who have transitioned to watch over my beloved pets who are on the other side.

Sum of the Parts

You've learned how to tap into your subconscious, turn up its volume, and lower the noise of your critical, conscious mind; this is all the process of preparing yourself to call upon the SoulSpirit to further support your subconscious and play big in your life.

As a way to go even deeper with this practice, you can expand your sense of time. From a young age, we're taught that time is linear, marching forward from the past, through the present, and into the future. We are also taught to respect the past and its lessons, savor the present for its experience, and prepare for the future.

But the truth is, time is not linear; it is spatial and boundless. And most of all, time is a form of perception. Take a look at the Time Continuum diagram on page 240.

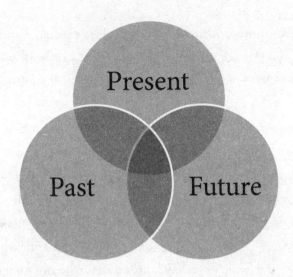

This image portrays the way your subconscious understands and senses time. Living in an endless present—the way we're often encouraged to—can undermine your mission of playing big and embracing the life you truly desire. Instead, let the past remain present in part. You can learn from the past to avoid repeating unproductive behaviors or patterns. At the same time, while staying mindful not to get stuck in the past, letting past mistakes or experiences define or constrain you.

Welcome the future into your present: look toward the future as a way to envision all that you want in your enlightened state. Looking forward, stay mindful of the context and reality of the past and present, and you will be creating a new ideal reality for yourself.

You are seeking a balance of three equal parts, learning to live in the center of the diagram, that powerful place where the past, present, and future become one. In this space, you can learn from the past, harness the energy of the present, and envision the future.

To deepen this understanding, the following exercise will reframe your experience of time and help you embrace the flow of energy and fluidity of time that occurs when you're connected to the SoulSpirit.

Hypnotic Hack: Time Travel

. . . .

This is an exercise in practicing moderation that will teach you to soften your gaze when you look at the past and toward the future. Let the past inform us. Let the future inspire us. The present is fleeting—it's gone in a split second.

1. Close your eyes and go within.
2. Bring to mind an event that didn't go well. Was it a bad date? A job that ended harshly?
3. Ask what your higher self wants you to learn from that event?
4. Energetically and lovingly lock in the lesson(s). They are yours forever.
5. Ask yourself, with these new lessons, how you will prevent this event from happening again in the future?

Flexibility and Fluidity

Just like time is a flexible concept and a subjective reality, staying connected to your subconscious and the SoulSpirit requires flexibility. You can practice fluidity to move from one time period to another, tracking the consistency of your true self. In each time period, you are still you. As you move further on this path of the present, staying at the center of the Time Continuum, you are creating a new future: a new and improved you. Life happens around you—events occur, environments change—yet you are still the ever-present you. At the spirit level, you remain constant; it's the conscious mind that's transformed through this process. The SoulSpirit and the Subconscious are your cornerstones and do not change. The more you practice the Six Principles of Subconscious Power, the more you will feel this inherent connection and place as home.

When you find yourself dwelling on the past, move back into the present. If you're looking too fast toward the future, move your eyes to something in your immediate concrete surroundings and tether yourself in the present. Even as you do so, recognize that the present shifts in a nanosecond. This means you are timeless.

As you hone this flexibility, you are learning how to travel through time. There's a reason they say the days go slow, but the years go fast. When you are in the present, you slow down time. When you remember the past, you speed up time. Time is a perception. Many clients will admit that they never felt like they belonged here, on this earth, until the Six Principles of Subconscious Power gave them room to move and feel free. The adoption of this universal place feels free because it's not circumstantial. It matters not where you were raised, where you lived, where in the world you to travel to. You take it with you because *it is you.*

A Final Message
from My Subconscious to Yours

Living a life connected to your subconscious is never boring. It asks that you give all that you have, everything you've got. It means setting bold expectations for yourself and following through. It means loving the people in your life passionately. It means believing in yourself and your dreams with your whole heart and soul. It means showing up every day with gusto and courage. It means expecting the exceptional.

As much as this sounds like living life full throttle, it's also playful and fun. It's a life filled with laughter, humor, and sass. Just as living your life this way calls for everything that you want, it also asks you not to take yourself so seriously—not because you're not worth it—but rather because it's important to keep yourself light, flexible, and in perspective. Just like me, you are only one person in a vast universe of swirling energy. We are each of the now and the forever.

You're at the end of the book, but this is just the beginning. In order to continue to build confidence and trust in yourself, maintain all that you've learned, check in with the Six Principles regularly, and continue to practice the Hypnotic Hacks to continuously tune into your subconscious and align it with your conscious mind. Remember the SoulSpirit and remember to call upon spirit energy and all your connections to the universe: that wave of light and vibration that protects you, fortifies you, and inspires you.

Your Daily Power Check-In

It's important to connect to the Six Principles on a regular basis, and I use this helpful quick guide every day. This exercise helps you quickly move through the Six Principles to energize and synthesize your mind, body, and spirit.

1. As always, begin by closing your eyes.
2. Find your self—your mind, body, and spirit—in the present moment and take mental note of where you are: establish your truth at this moment in time.
3. Connect with your subconscious and quickly assess if it is in alignment with your conscious mind; if not, send energy to restore balance and call upon the SoulSpirit to mend the fracture.
4. Orient your subconscious toward others in your energetic circle; move toward or away to establish or reinforce the integrity of your subconscious–conscious mind connection.
5. Utilize your inner judgment and examine your place, your relations, your goals, and your desires; ascertain if all in your life manifests goodness of fit for your subconscious.
6. Give to yourself and to those in your energetic circle of influence in proper amount to set up give to get proportionally and fairly.
7. Scan your body for feelings of strength and/or vulnerability. If you notice any specific issues coming to light, take note and address them early, using the advice in part 2 as needed.
8. Continue to play big in both immediate endeavors and long-term pursuits.

   I use this cheat sheet on a daily basis to remind me of all that exists at my literal fingertips. We know that regardless of our situations in life, each day can bring equal amounts of joy and stress. Indeed, stress is an inevitable feature of life on this planet. I choose not to fight it, but instead relax into the very truth of it. In fact, more and more scientists and medical doctors are looking at ways not to avoid stress but to work with it. And that's what the Six Principles are all about: making the most of our time here, having fun, and learning what we are here to learn.

Your Subconscious Life

It's my greatest wish that you discover your subconscious power so that you may experience all that you are. Yes, we all have the potential to change, grow, and continue to adapt with resilience and courage. But what if resilience didn't require so much work, pain, or heartache? That's one of the biggest, most important keys of *Subconscious Power*—it's easy. Now enjoy!

References

Chapter 1

Michael A. Hunter et al., "Functional Connectivity Within and Between Intrinsic Brain Networks Correlates with Trait Mind Wandering," *Neuropsychologia* 103 (August 2017): 140–53.

Biography of Milton Erickson, https://www.erickson-foundation.org/biography/.

Daniel Goleman and Richard J. Davidson, *Altered Traits: Science Reveals How Meditation Changes Your Mind, Brain, and Body* (New York: Avery, 2017).

Antonio R. Damasio, "Descartes' Error and the Future of Human Life," *Scientific American* 271, no. 144 (1994).

Richard J. Davidson and Sharon Begley, *The Emotional Life of Your Brain: How Its Unique Patterns Affect the Way You Think, Feel, and Live—and How You Can Change Them* (New York: Hudson Street Press, 2012).

Jon Kabat-Zinn, *Full Catastrophe Living: Using the Wisdom of Your Body and Mind to Face Stress, Pain, and Illness* (New York: Bantam Books, 2013).

Steven Jay Lynn et al., "Hypnosis as an Empirically Supported Clinical Intervention: The State of the Evidence and a Look to the Future," *International Journal of Clinical and Experimental Hypnosis* 48, no. 2 (2000): 239–59.

Chapter 2

Deepak Chopra, *Perfect Health: The Complete Mind/Body Guide* (New York: Harmony, 1991).

Louise Hay, *Heal Your Body: The Mental Causes for Physical Illness and the Metaphysical Way to Overcome Them*, 4th ed. (Carlsbad, CA: Hay House, 1984).

Chapter 4

Charles Darwin, *On the Origin of Species by Means of Natural Selection, or Preservation of Favoured Races in the Struggle for Life* (London: John Murray, 1859).

Joseph E. LeDoux, *The Emotional Brain: The Mysterious Underpinnings of Emotional Life* (New York: Simon & Schuster, 1996).

Antonio R. Damasio, *Descartes' Error: Emotion, Reason, and the Human Brain* (New York: G. P. Putnam, 1994).

Antonio R. Damasio, *Self Comes to Mind: Constructing the Conscious Brain* (New York: Pantheon/Random House, 2010).

Chapter 5

W. Schultz, P. Dayan, and P. R. Montague, "A Neural Substrate of Prediction and Reward," *Science* 275 (1997): 1593–99.

David M. Amodio, "The Neuroscience of Prejudice and Stereotyping," *Nature Review Neuroscience* 15, no. 10 (2014): 670–81.

Mahzarin R. Banaji et al., "How (Un)ethical Are You?," *Harvard Business Review*, December 2003: 5, 58–60.

Anthony G. Greenwald et al., "Statistically Small Effects of the Implicit Association Test Can Have Societally Large Effects," *Journal of Personality and Social Psychology* 108, no. 4 (2015): 553–61.

A. Bechara, H. Damasio, D. Tranel, and A.R. Damasio, "Deciding Advantageously Before Knowing the Advantageous Strategy," *Science* 275 (1997): 1293–95.

Daniel Kahneman, *Thinking, Fast and Slow* (New York: Farrar, Straus and Giroux, 2011).

Anthony G. Greenwald, Debbie E. McGhee, and Jordan L. K. Schwartz, "Measuring Individual Differences in Implicit Cognition: The Implicit Association Test," *Journal of Personality and Social Psychology* 74, no. 6 (1998): 1464–80.

Gavin de Becker, *The Gift of Fear* (New York: Dell Publishing, 1997).

J. Wood, *Interpersonal Communication: Everyday Encounters* (Boston: Wadsworth-Cengage Learning, 2001).

Paul Ekman, William V. Friesen, and Peter Ellsworth, *Emotion in the Human Face: Guidelines for Research and an Integration of Findings* (New York: Pergamon Press, 1972).

Charles Darwin, *The Expression of the Emotions in Man and Animals* (Chicago: University of Chicago Press, 1965).

Amy Cuddy, *Presence: Bringing Your Boldest Self to Your Biggest Challenges* (New York: Little, Brown and Company, 2015).

Brian A. Primack et al., "The Association Between Valence of Social Media Experiences and Depressive Symptoms," *Depression and Anxiety* 35, no. 8 (2018): 784–94.

Ramin Mojtabai, Mark Olfson, and Beth Han, "National Trends in the Prevalence and Treatment of Depression in Adolescents and Young Adults," *Pediatrics*, November 2016.

Chapter 6

Sarah Brosnan and Frans de Waal, "Monkeys Reject Unequal Pay." *Nature* 425, no. 6955 (September 2003): 297–9.

Chapter 7

Shel Silverstein, *The Giving Tree* (New York: Harper & Row, 1964).

Seamus Heaney, *The Spirit Level* (New York: Farrar, Strauss and Giroux, 1996).

Marianne Williamson, *A Return to Love* (New York: HarperCollins, 1992).

Chapter 8

Louise Hay, *Heal Your Body: The Mental Causes for Physical Illness and the Metaphysical Way to Overcome Them*, 4th ed. (Carlsbad, CA: Hay House, 1984).

Lori Neighbors and Jeffrey Sobal, "Weight and Weddings: Women's Weight Ideals and Weight Management Behaviors for Their Wedding Day," *Appetite* 50, no. 2–3 (March–May 2008): 550–54.

William Bennett, MD, and Joel Gurin, *The Dieter's Dilemma* (New York: Basic Books, 1982).

Craig M. Hales et al., "Trends in Obesity and Severe Obesity Prevalence in US Youth and Adults by Sex and Age, 2007–2008 to 2015–2016," *JAMA* 319, no. 16 (2018): 1723–25.

Gitanjali M. Singh et al., "Estimated Global, Regional, and National Disease Burdens Related to Sugar-Sweetened Beverage Consumption in 2010," Circulation 132, no. 8 (2015): 639–66.

Don Gerrard, *One Bowl: A Guide to Eating for Body and Spirit* (New York: Marlowe & Co., 2001).

Acknowledgments

No book is written alone, and *Subconscious Power* is not an exception. I would like to extend my most soulful gratitude to the following remarkable women and men:

Thanks to Claudia Riemer Boutote at Red Raven Studio for her publishing and marketing expertise; Claudia acted on her power to attract and lives her life by these principles. She's naturally and effortlessly gracious, delicate, and illuminating. Without Claudia, this book would not exist; all of the readers' lives it will elevate can send her an intentional "thank you" with thought language. Claudia is both giver and receiver, moving mountains with her talent.

Yfat Reiss Gendell, my super-agent, is the single most impressive woman I have ever met. Her ability to frame a situation into a positive light-form is remarkable. Her pace is record speed and her action warps steel, all in a delicate supermodel exterior. I'm in complete awe of Yfat! She's the most unique balance of all magnificent things.

Billie Fitzpatrick, my writing partner, who I loved the minute I saw her beaming face and quick smile. She looks exactly like warm pancakes taste. Working alongside Billie was a sprint while smelling the roses. Her curiosity is endless, her resourcefulness fresh, and her ability to absorb my thoughts, ideas, and feelings remarkable. She's a translator of spirit and divine intelligence.

Sarah Pelz, Atria editor extraordinaire, whose editing had us dig deep into what we know and whose torch illuminated the way. With her soft touch, steady hand, and solid intention, she took us in and loved us all the way to print. I send my gratitude to her for this blessed experience, nurturing us and standing in the light so bright we could find her. She is both a star and a star maker.

Marianne Williamson, author and spirit shepherd, who predicted I would write this book. I keenly remember the day when she energetically set it in motion, and here we are! She is completely fascinating; an ethereal beauty, a modern-day visionary in rock 'n' roll leather pants!

Shelley Stockwell Nicholas, PhD, author and president of the International Hypnosis Federation, has been a soul-colleague for years. To me she's not only the lighthouse of Palos Verdes, but of the world. Her bubbly way is intoxicating, and her enormous heart compassionate. Fifty pounds ago, Shelley hypnotized my husband, Brad, bringing him to his physical greatness and stamina. We are just a few of the many who have benefited from her techniques and brilliance.

Dick Sutphen, PhD, author and president of the American Board of Hypnotherapy and my go-to for water in the well. Dick's depth of understanding is unsurpassed. As my personal hypnotist, he's brought forth the best I have to give, time and time again.

Brian L. Weiss, MD, author of the iconic *Many Lives, Many Masters*, facilitated my very first experience with hypnosis. He was the sole reason I began to explore the protocol. His quick wit, bravery, and dedication to what he knows have inspired me throughout my career.

Scott Kudia, PhD, author of *If This Is Love, Why Am I Unhappy?*, is my mirror-image colleague in enthusiasm for the potential of the human spirit. He believes in healing, sanctity of spirit, and boundless levels of achievement. His never-wavering energy and optimism are the best nest to land in.

Sidney Dinow, my confidant and mentor, has saved my life in many ways. He appeared at a time I needed guidance and a heart to melt into.

He is stoic and soft, honest and reassuring. I know we've known each other before, and I pray we'll continue to connect; his dancing blue eyes I'd know in any lifetime.

My Novecento family, my soul-sisters and brothers, who exude gratitude, beauty, and wisdom. Alex and Melika are stars. They're luminous and attract the best for all of us. Who else offers their kidney in case you should ever need one? Melika's mom, Priscilla and Chris, Bobby and Marina, Michele, Freddy and Tina, with all their beautiful babies, are pure love; I'm blessed to call them family.

My clients—past, present, and future—who inspire me every day to truly nurture and listen to the power of the subconscious. You are my rock stars!

To all, thank you!

Index

About the Author

Kimberly Friedmutter, CHt, is a world-renowned board-certified hypnotherapist who works with some of Hollywood's best-known luminaries, titans of industry, leaders, and influencers around the globe. Kimberly is a member of the prestigious UCLA Health System Board, the American Board of Hypnotherapy, the International Hypnosis Federation, and the Association for Integrative Psychology. She is also a Certified Master Hypnotist and a Certified NLP Trainer. Previously, Kimberly was the popular host of a top-rated talk radio program and held prominent positions in the entertainment, fashion, and media industries. She is currently in private practice and divides her time between Nevada and California, serving high-performing clientele who share her philosophy, "Expect the Exceptional." Visit kimberly friedmutter.com.